WHAT PEOPLE ARE SAYING

"Philip Cohen's raw authenticity and vulnerability take the reader on a journey into the ravages of brokenness and abandonment. This book is for those whose hopes and dreams seem continually shattered beyond repair. Are you stuck in cycles of addiction, mood swings, acting out, or depression? If so, please read this book to the end. There is hope. Jesus does shine through, and He is shining through to you right now."

GREG SMITH - Director of Outreach, New Horizons Foundation Inc., Colorado Springs, Colorado

"This book caused me to really ponder John 14:6 passage again! My life was proof enough for me that one's search for the truth will ultimately lead them to Jesus. Phil's willingness to bear his soul confirms my conviction! I could feel his soul searching for truth through abuse, poverty, rejection, drugs, loneliness, confusion, family, wealth, and even religion. *Jesus Shines Through* is emotionally challenging to read, but you are compelled to continue until the end. You want to know where this life's journey is going. The end will leave you thankful and give you courage to continue your journey of discovering the truth! *Jesus Shines Through* for all who seek the truth no matter where you begin your journey, or where it leads you along the way. Phil, thank you for sharing with us! I am blessed by your transparency. My hope has increased, my faith has been strengthened, and I am more confident in the matchless love of Jesus for all!"

CLAUDE L. BENNETT, JR. - Founder, Heaven on Earth Ministries Saint Louis, Missouri

"Phil Cohen is an honest man with a pure heart. These pages are filled with memories. Some good, and others — not so good. *Jesus Shines Through* is the abiding theme of Phil's life. In the depths of despair, Jesus shines through. In the heights of accomplishment, Jesus shines through. In the doldrums of daily life, Jesus shines through. Humans have an innate understanding that life is about so much more than punching-in and punching-out. Some seek solace in spirituality, while others pursue self-actualization. The tireless wondering always leads back to the origin: We were made by God, in His image, for communion with Him, and to His glory. As you read this story, my prayer for you is that you would find the Truth. That your eyes would see Jesus shining through."

PETER HARTZELL - **Founder & President,**
Tree House Media, LLC.

"Your story shines a light into the dark and emptiness of a lifestyle without God, the despair and oppression of religion without relationship, and the constant, relentless love of our heavenly father, who will never stop pursuing our heart.

The writing style is very captivating and definitely makes you curious to what will happen next. Also, very easy to read. And the truth Jesus showed you about seeing each person as created in his beautiful image instead of through religious cautions is powerful! Thank you for the genuine invitation to meet Jesus at the end. I believe this will impact the hearts and lives of many."

JOHN DETWILER - **General Manager, Detwiler Roofing, LLC**

"The Cohen's remarkable journey epitomizes The Providence of God. God's caring provision for Phil and Gina as He guided their journey of faith through life, accomplishing His purpose in them, is the story, Jesus Shines Through.

Their childhood lives were complete opposites. The heartbreaking events of Phil's childhood survival, in a dysfunctional, violent, abusive home, as told in Jesus Shines Through, left him feeling worthless, angry, disillusioned, alone and looking for a place to belong. Gina's secure upper class, safe environment left her courageous, adventurous, and eager to break free to find herself in the world of the 70's. Two most unlikely candidates for a lasting faith in Jesus, a marriage commitment that has survived over 40 years and produced nine amazingly gifted and talented children.

Wherever your life has led you, reading this book will give you hope in a Creator who is in control even in the chaos of life. He makes Beauty from Ashes."

LINDA K. ROBERTS - And It Came To Pass,
All American Enterprises

"I so appreciated your passion for Jesus over many decades. You remained steadfast in your pursuit of Him even through many trials in your life. Jesus indeed shines through your book, and my hope and prayer is it will lead many to seek Him. I love your writing style. I found the book to be a real page turner.

I so appreciated you seeing Jesus shining through in many people throughout your life. Protestants and others often bash Catholics, but the unconditional love and joy in my wife's Catholic family helped draw me to want what they had! And Jesus continues to shine through them today and to impact my life. I hope to have rabbis and others see the peace, joy, and love in my heart and that I can leave my judgments at the cross. I pray for your eyesight and trust that God will continue to use you."

JIM ADLER - ADLER & MANSON, LC Attorneys at Law

"As I am someone also from a toxic Jewish home, in NYC, I can relate. Then we both got into the hippy life and into joyful Christian experience, then legalistic Christianity, then recovery. Your transparent recounting of all your trauma and subsequent searching was riveting. Your experience of the amazing joy of salvation in Messiah, which causes lifelong transformation, was what I can TOTALLY relate to.

However, your life in the world of Christian legalism was also much stronger than mine, although similarly my holiness people thought of themselves as the real Christians. I love how the Mennonites talked about your intensity. Jewish people tend to be intense. We are like a spring of spiritual energy that has been wound and cocked and suppressed for 2000 years. I'm soooo glad that you finally found healing and joy in Messiah in the wider evangelical world!"

SHMUEL WOLKENFIELD – Senior Rabbi, Or HaOlam Messianic Synagogue, Kansas City, Missouri

JESUS SHINES THROUGH

A LIFELONG SEARCH THROUGH HIPPIES, COMMUNES, RAGE, AND CHURCH CULTURE FOR THE GOD WHO HEALS

PHILLIP COHEN

Carpenter's Son Publishing

Franklin, Tennessee

www.Healthy-leaders.com
www.JesusShinesThrough.com

Published by Carpenter's Son Publishing
Franklin, Tennessee

ISBN 978-1-954437-98-2

Ebook ISBN 978-1-956370-03-4

Edited by Bob Irvin

Cover and Interior Design by Suzanne Lawing

Printed in the United States of America

CONTENTS

Introduction and Apology 9

Chapter 1   A Cradle of Violence 13

Chapter 2   Uncle Bert 19

Chapter 3   More Terror 23

Chapter 4   "Coin, You're a Dud" 31

Chapter 5   Bar Mitzvah, Barely 41

Chapter 6   Downward Spiral 47

Chapter 7   Mexico 57

Chapter 8   Wally 67

Chapter 9   Aimless 75

Chapter 10   Nomad 83

Chapter 11   Rejection 89

Chapter 12   Primal Screams and Peace
Under the Waterfall 97

Chapter 13   Little Country Church 107

Chapter 14   The Prodigal 115

Chapter 15   Restitution and Reconciliation 121

Chapter 16   Crossroads 131

Chapter 17   Finding God and Myself in the Pigpen . . . 135

Chapter 18   They Wouldn't Even Let
Me Say Goodbye 141

Chapter 19   Newlyweds 147

Chapter 20   Outcast 155

Chapter 21   The Heart of a Craftsman 165

Chapter 22   Darkness in the Church,
Light Shining in My Business 171

Chapter 23   A Song for God. 179

Chapter 24   A New Beginning .187

Chapter 25   Night Sessions. 195

Chapter 26   Hope in the Jungle. 203

Chapter 27   A Wounded Healer. 211

Chapter 28:   Escape by Night 217

Chapter 29   The Exodus 225

Chapter 30   Steve, We Loved You. 229

Chapter 31:   A Reluctant Leader. 233

Chapter 32   The Greater Honor 239

Chapter 33   "What's Your Purpose?" 245

Epilogue   Jesus Shines Through 253

INTRODUCTION AND APOLOGY

In some ways my story is historical:

- I grow up in inner-city Chicago, Atlanta, and Miami in the 1950s and '60s in a violent and dysfunctional Jewish home in a hurting, anti-Semitic, post-World War II world.

- In the late '60s and early '70s I become deeply immersed in the hippie movement along with millions of people my age who are searching for peace and love, many of us saturating ourselves with drugs, loud music, sex, and violence.

- I spend twenty-six years in heavy-handed Christian fundamentalist communities, isolated from the rest of the world, beginning my married life in poverty in one of the poorest counties in the U.S.

- All of that has become the reason for my lifelong search for people who truly love each other and the journey inside myself to find healing from the inner pain that keeps me from knowing love.

I'm telling my story the best I can, asking God to help me write it. I'm not trying to conceal or excuse the role I've played in my own troubles. I see myself as a struggling, stumbling sinner, one who's trying to sort out the real, healing, and loving God from the many fake gods that offer much but deliver little.

Perhaps you'll discover parts of yourself or someone you know in this book.

I don't expect you to agree with everything here. Hey, I don't always agree with myself. I'm sure once this book is published, I'll still be trying to understand life more clearly from God's perspective.

Nothing written here is intended to harm anyone. I have no ax to grind. Although we spent twenty-six years in a conservative Mennonite church, what happened to us can happen in many other churches.

As Mark Bishop writes:

God builds churches
With broken people
With hurting people
With searching people
And somehow these imperfect people
Find strength to make it through
And the broken become brand new.

(Lyrics are from "God Builds Churches with Broken People," written by Mark Bishop. Copyright Possum Run Music, Chris White Music, Asheville Music.)

I'm trusting that, while my painful experiences have brought me closer to Jesus—whenever I've been willing to take his way through the pain—the right and wrong roles I've played in other people's lives also are working to bring them come closer to Jesus.

This book has taken more than 10 years and hundreds of hours to write. A team of writers and editors have combed through every chapter, sentence, and phrase multiple times to ensure the story is accurate and easy to read. To experience the greatest blessing, I invite you to start at the beginning and read all the way to the end.

One more thing: I'm writing my story in present tense. I've discovered that when I write in past tense, I'm telling my story as I remember it. But when I switch to present tense, I'm reliving the scenes of my life, as though I'm actually there. I see more details. I feel more feelings. I pray that's your experience too.

So there's my short introduction. Now welcome to my story. May your life be enriched.

Phillip Cohen
July 2023

Chapter 1

A CRADLE OF VIOLENCE

"Jerry, stop it! Stop!"

I burrow under the covers and pull the pillow over my head, trying to block out the ugly sounds on the other side of the wall.

"Stop it!" Mom's screams cut through the night and stab my heart. Trembling uncontrollably, I clutch the pillow more tightly around my ears, but I can't block the screams of my parents fighting in the next room.

"Bernice, you're worthless! Go ahead and leave me! There's not a man in the world who would want you. Nobody could possibly love you!"

My 10-year-old body involuntarily stiffens every time Dad spits out another insult, and I flinch at the dull sound of his fist hitting my mother's face and body.

I squeeze my eyes shut but can't block the horrifying images from my mind. I've heard so many vicious fights between them—rather, my father beating my mother—that I don't need to be there to know what's happening.

That desperate gurgling sound? Mom is struggling to breathe as Dad chokes her. In my mind, I see his strong hands wrapped around her neck, squeezing tighter and tighter, choking her into unwilling submission.

"Somebody . . . please . . . help me!"

Thud! Thud!

It's not enough for him to choke her; Dad repeatedly slams her head into the wall.

I curl into a ball and fight against the darkness engulfing me. When the noise fades, the silence terrifies me even more. *Has Dad finally killed Mom?* I become perfectly still, and I stop breathing while my ears strain for a sign that my mother's still alive. The night is silent except for an occasional car passing by on our Chicago street.

Tightly clenching my teeth, I push all the fear and sadness into my soul. My chest heaves as silent screams explode inside. Still, my eyes and mouth remain tightly shut, stifling my cries and tears.

The door bursts open, and Dad storms into my bedroom.

"Daddy, please!" I cry and beg for mercy, but it's no use. Fueled by a toxic mix of prescription pain pills and Scotch, Dad is in a full-blown rage. Grabbing my arm, he yanks me from the bed. With one strong hand he drags me into the living room. His other hand drunkenly fumbles with his belt, trying to snap it free from his trousers.

"You're a baby!" Dad snarls as he raises the belt above his head. "Quit crying, or I'll give you something to cry about!"

Thud!

As the first blow lands, I realize it's not the sharp sting of leather but the thud of the metal buckle. When Dad's mildly drunk, he whips me with the leather end of the belt on the parts of my body you can't see when I have my clothes on. When he falls off the deep end, he flails wildly without caring where he hits me.

As Dad repeatedly slams me with his belt buckle, I collapse to the floor and curl into a fetal position, my arms crossed over my face. It's no use. The heavy buckle slamming into my arms hurts so badly that

I jerk my hands away and let the next blows hit my face. The pain makes me instinctively throw up my hands again to ward off the next blow.

When Dad's exhausted from beating me, he staggers from the room, leaving my face and arms bruised and throbbing painfully. Not wanting to attract Dad's attention, I muffle my sobs. I hear Mom moving in the next room; at least she's still alive. With this bit of hope, I creep into bed and try to sleep so I can forget the horror of my life for a few hours.

* * * * *

When I wake up in the morning, last night's events are like a hazy dream, a nightmare to be forgotten in the light of a new day. But the moment I stir, the pain in my forearms reminds me it wasn't a dream. I stumble into the bathroom and look in the mirror. Ugly black and blue bruises on my face testify to the damage done by Dad's heavy belt buckle.

I shuffle into the kitchen in my footie pajamas, stepping across an empty whiskey bottle in the doorway. The dishes on the counter are stained with last night's dried spaghetti sauce, and the floor needs sweeping. I hardly notice the chaos, though. It's just too familiar and normal.

Mom sits at the kitchen table with her nightgown pulled tightly around her bony shoulders, looking even worse than I feel. Her face and neck are bruised. She winces as she touches a bruise on her neck. Silent tears trickle down her face and drip onto the checkered tablecloth.

I remember when I was around 4 years old, I woke up in the middle of the night, afraid to die. Mom came in, placed me on her lap, held me close, and said, "You're not going to die. You're going to grow up, become a man, get married, and have children and grandchildren. Then after you've lived a good life, you're going to die and go to Heaven."

Now she looks at me with dull, empty, and lifeless eyes. I shift uneasily. Mom is a broken wretch of misery. Before either of us speaks, Dad appears in the kitchen, ready to head to work. He gazes at our bruises with a disgusted look on his face.

"Phillip, you're not going to school like that," he says. "You need to stay home. If you go outside today, wear sunglasses, and if anyone asks you what happened, tell them you fell down the stairs."

Nodding wordlessly, I pour cereal and milk into my bowl. I know the drill. I wonder if the neighbors heard the commotion last night.

Dad somehow manages to keep his good reputation in our middle-class Jewish neighborhood. When he steps out the front door, impeccably dressed and groomed, the neighbors assume the Jerry Cohen they know is a kindhearted, hardworking gentleman. They know only the suave and helpful man with a rising career at the airline. Mom and I know the other Jerry Cohen, the monster who fuels his demons with Scotch and prescription pain pills.

Despite all the beatings I suffer from his hands, I'm loyal to my dad. Even without his threats, I'm more than willing to lie about my bruises to protect his reputation. And I don't care about missing school. Today I can hang out—alone—at the park playground at the end of our street.

* * * * *

Later that morning, I'm sitting on a swing in the park, aimlessly tracing patterns on the ground with my shoe, thinking about my father. He's a handsome man who takes endless pains to preserve his image and good looks. I often watch him standing in front of the mirror, combing and brushing his wavy black locks. Scissors in hand, he examines every hair on his head and his Clark Gable mustache, clipping away any hair that's gray or out of place.

Dad always wears nice suits, spit-shined shoes, and a fresh manicure with clear nail polish. Our extended family, neighbors, and business associates view Dad as a gentleman, although one with perpetually bad luck, especially with money. For example, the grocery store he and Mom owned in Gary, Indiana, when I was 5 years old had been robbed a few times and gone bankrupt. Then Dad got a job working for Northwest Airlines at Chicago's Midway Airport. On one of his 90-mile commutes to work, a train slammed into his car and wrapped it around a nearby power pole.

Although he escaped with minor injuries, I think that's when Dad got hooked on painkillers. During his recovery he convinced himself and his doctors he's "allergic to pain"—those are his exact words. His doctors keep giving him prescriptions for strong sedatives, which he combines with whiskey, creating the volatile mixture that fuels his outbursts. Despite all the pain I suffer from his intoxicated eruptions, I won't admit Dad's an alcoholic. Dad shares my denial; if Mom or I hint he has a drinking problem, he verbally attacks us like a vicious monster.

I don't know much about Dad's childhood except that Grandpa Phil (the man I was named after) often beat Dad and Grandma Mary. They were very poor, receiving welfare from the synagogue in inner-city Chicago where Dad grew up. Dad tells stories about stealing gumball machines for the money in them and stealing bread from the local bakery.

Grandpa Phil died at age 41 from a massive heart attack. Dad wasn't there when Grandpa Phil died—he was aboard a Navy ship somewhere near Japan during World War II. Dad never seemed to come through mourning his father's death. Dad has had multiple nervous breakdowns, with several stays in mental hospitals. It always seems to point back to *his* dad. One psychiatrist tells Dad he still hates his father. Another tells Dad he really loves his father. None of this seems to tame the horrible demons that torment him.

Dad is the oldest son. Uncle Bert was born a few years later. The family talks sometimes about Harold, Bert's twin, who died when he was around six months old. Many years later I'll learn that Grandpa Phil accidentally killed Harold—he shook him until he died. It's a family secret until Grandma Mary agonizingly reveals what actually happened many years later when she's on her deathbed.

As I ponder these mysteries, I twist myself around on the playground swing, then release myself to spin madly as the ropes unwind. The dizzying feeling spins me into a dark, bottomless abyss, replicating the nausea I feel during Dad's violent outbursts.

Occasionally, after a night of berating and beating Mom, me, or both of us, Dad apologizes. When I close my eyes against the dizziness, I see Dad crying and begging us to forgive him. More than once he promises to change, saying that things will get better. The first few times he promises, I dare to hope he'll change, but harsh reality soon teaches me it's not going to happen. Despite his good intentions, alcohol and pills suck him back into the only world he knows—one of tormented violence.

The more desperate and frustrated he becomes, the harder the demons hit him, and the harder he strikes out at those who love him.

Far from a sanctuary of comfort and security, our home is a house of horrors. So I'm relieved to spend this day in the park, away from the house where anger, fear, and pain are the only reality we know.

Chapter 2

UNCLE BERT

Dad's brother Bert is my only uncle and the lone bright spot in my childhood. No other adult loves and accepts me unconditionally, and I adore him in return. Our special bond began way back when I was just a toddler. He lives a few miles from our house, and sometimes he comes over just to see me. When he returned from serving in the Korean War, he came by to let me admire him in his crisp Army dress uniform. And one night he woke me up so I could meet Audrey, his beautiful wife-to-be.

Best of all, Uncle Bert has given me a special nickname. He calls me Flip, and my little heart flips with joy whenever he says my name. Unlike Dad, who ignores me unless he's upset with me, Uncle Bert frequently takes time to get on my level, look me in the eye, and address me as an equal.

One day as I rush to greet him with my usual hug and kiss, Uncle Bert says, "Flip, you're getting too big for that. You'll be a man someday. It's time to shake hands like a man."

He reaches out his strong hand. I place my limp hand in his.

"Hey, not like that!" he says with a loving smile. "That's a dead fish. Be firm and friendly."

His giant hand swallows mine as he squeezes it so hard I drop to my knees with my mouth twisted in a grimace.

He relaxes his grip. I stand up straight, take a deep breath, clench my teeth, and squeeze his hand with all my six-year-old strength.

"G-r-r-r," I snarl, standing on tiptoes for extra leverage.

Uncle Bert grins and nods approvingly while he squeezes back so hard that I sink to the floor once more.

"Ow! That hurts!"

"But you did it!" Uncle Bert says. "You shook hands like a man." He looks into my eyes with a broad grin and love as wide as the sky. I beam from his praise.

Uncle Bert and I understand each other. Sometimes when his family and ours get together, we pair up to play Password. Each pair of players faces each other across the table, and the players on one side draw a card from the deck with a word on it. Those players then give their partners a one-word clue. The first partner to correctly guess the original word wins a point for their team.

When Uncle Bert and I pair up, we read each other's minds.

"Flip, pay close attention," Uncle Bert says during one of the games. "The word is *poetry*."

"Prose," I immediately say.

"Hey, that's it!" Uncle Bert cheers. I'm incredibly proud because I just learned that word in school the week before.

"I don't know how you two do it," Aunt Audrey says, shaking her head admiringly. "Why do the rest of us even bother? You two always win."

"It's because we think alike," I say proudly. Uncle Bert gives me a sly wink and a grin.

Dad and Uncle Bert are so unalike it's hard to believe they're brothers. Dad frequently tells me I'll never amount to anything and I'll die

Dad frequently tells me I'll never amount to anything and I'll die in a gutter. Uncle Bert believes I'll succeed. In fact, he takes lots of time to make sure I succeed.

in a gutter. Uncle Bert believes I'll succeed. In fact, he takes lots of time to make sure I succeed.

For example, I've been assigned to give a sales presentation in a high school class. Uncle Bert spends hours coaching me. "Always leave an impression, Flip, even if you have to pee on the wall."

Okay, Uncle Bert, I get your point, I think. *You left an impression.*

The teacher is impressed with my presentation and asks me to repeat it for another class while he records it for a future teaching aid.

It's a rare moment for me to do well in school. Dad has given me many beatings for receiving poor grades. He constantly shames me because he says I have a good mind but don't use it. Whenever I get poor grades on my report card—which is practically every semester—he makes me stay in the house every day after school and study. However, I don't study; I have an open textbook in front of me, but I'm staring at a comic book.

Uncle Bert never mentions Dad's abuse, but I'm sure he at least suspects something's going on. Although Dad tries hard to protect his gentleman's image, he surely must be leaving visible clues to someone as close to us as Uncle Bert.

Chapter 3

MORE TERROR

One evening, Dad comes home from work in a foul mood. He glares at the stew Mom has cooked on the stove, then turns on her.

"What makes you think I want a hot meal on a hot day?" he demands. "I come home from work hot and sweaty. Why would I want to heat myself even more with stupid stew? You know better than that!"

"How am I supposed to read your mind?" Mom yells back at Dad. "If I had a cold supper, you would insist on a hot meal. I never know when you'll get home, and you don't tell me what you want, so I fix something I can keep warm on the stove."

The muscles and veins on Dad's jaw bulge as he balls his fists and moves toward Mom.

"Get away from me!" Mom screams, quickly retreating behind the table and beyond his reach.

Dad grabs the table's edge and leans across it, glaring at her. Then he springs around and rushes at her, but Mom dodges his clutching hands. As she circles the table with Dad in close pursuit, Mom snatches a butcher knife from a drawer and hurls it at Dad.

It's like I'm watching the scene in slow motion. Dad steps aside as the knife flies past him, heading straight toward me. I catch the blade between my elbow and ribcage and stand rigid for a moment, too frightened to see if I've been stabbed.

I don't feel any warm blood. As I relax my elbow, the knife clatters to the floor. The blade somehow, in some way, did not penetrate skin. I look up, expecting Dad and Mom to show some shock, relief—*something*—but neither of them notices.

They're still fighting when Mom bolts across the living room, headed for the door. Dad grabs the door, slams Mom against the wall, and swings the door into her face. Mom struggles to get free. Dad pulls the door back and slams it into Mom's face again, smashing her head against the wall and breaking her nose.

Screaming in pain and terror, she runs out of the house.

Dad shuts the door, glares through the small window, and whispers, "Go ahead, get out of here!" Turning from the door, he makes a dismissive wave and mutters, "Good riddance."

Afraid I'm Dad's next target, I duck into my room. I'm not breathing as I wait for what's next. Dad mutters something as he shuffles into the kitchen, where he's probably taking a swig from his beloved bottle of Scotch. I'm relieved he's not coming after me. Squeezing my eyes shut, I try to retreat into my imaginary place. In that place, our home is quiet and peaceful, my parents love each other, and my dad plays catch with me in the yard.

Fresh waves of panic hit as I realize Mom is gone. Now I have to take care of my baby brother Eddie and my three-year-old sister Diane until she returns. But what if she never returns? Who's going to take care of us?

A couple of hours later the doorbell rings. Dad opens the front door.

"Mr. Cohen." A deep male voice interrupts the silence. "We found your wife's car parked on a railroad track. She was lying on the front seat, waiting for the train."

Mom wants to kill herself! She wants to die and leave Diane, Eddie, and me alone in this hell house. Shuddering uncontrollably, I tiptoe into the living room, where Mom stands in the middle of the room, shoulders slumped, head drooping in shame. My sweet, beautiful mother's face is caked with dried blood and masked in so much pain.

"Thank you, officer." Dad responds smoothly. "She's a little disturbed." He taps his temple to indicate Mom is crazy. "I'll take good care of her."

The officer looks emotionlessly at my dad for a moment, then turns and walks toward his car. Dad closes the door and turns on Mom.

"You can't even kill yourself!" he hisses with a malicious sneer. "You knew parking your car on the tracks would draw attention. Why didn't you just lie down in front of the train and do it right?"

Mom darts into the bathroom and locks the door. Dad chuckles as though he's won his game. Mom remains in the bathroom for a long time. I hear water running in the sink and drawers opening and closing.

I'm tired. I think tonight's drama is finally over and I can go to bed. Just then Mom bursts from the bathroom, calls Dad an ugly name, and throws an empty pill bottle at him. Her words are slurred, her eyes glazed, and she sways unsteadily.

Dad picks up the pill bottle, reads the label, and shakes it—it's empty.

"You swallowed the whole bottle of sleeping pills!" he screams.

Mom's knees buckle as she collapses. Dad grabs a mug of leftover coffee, forces her lips open, and pours the cold liquid into her mouth.

Mom coughs and sputters, spraying coffee while Dad slaps her face and yells at her to wake up. He drags her against the wall and into a sitting position and shoves his palm into her stomach, trying to make her throw up the pills. It's no use, and at last he half-carries her limp form out the door to the car. The engine starts, the car drives away, and I assume Dad is taking her to the hospital.

Too exhausted to think, I drop into bed and fall asleep.

The next morning, Mom and Dad are at home, and both act as though nothing unusual has happened. They don't talk about Mom's suicide attempt or the hospital. Although we all pretend nothing has happened, my insides know something is very, very wrong.

* * * * *

During one of his unpredictable good moods, Dad decides to play with me. That's what dads do, right? Only my dad doesn't know how to play with a four-year-old boy, so he's like a wild animal. Like a male lion dominating his cub, he wrestles me to the floor and sits on my chest, pinning my arms to the floor with his strong hands.

At first, I'm laughing at our little game. Then Dad licks my face over and over.

"Stop!" I plead as his weight squeezes my chest and I can't breathe. "I don't want to play!"

"You don't like this?" Dad's tone is mocking me. "You don't like to play?"

"Stop it!" I beg again, but Dad continues laughing and licking my face as I writhe and struggle to escape his grip. I hear Mom pleading with Dad, but I'm struggling too hard to understand what she's saying.

Finally Dad stands up straight and looks at my contorted face in disgust. "You're a baby!" he sneers. "You don't even know how to play!"

I gasp for air when he gets off my chest, but the nightmare isn't over yet.

"Stand up!" he barks, and I shakily pull myself to my feet, my nose wrinkling at the unpleasant odor of saliva on my face.

"If you want to cry, I'll give you something to cry about. Turn around and touch your toes," Dad orders, and I mutely obey. He pulls his belt from his trousers and . . . *crack!* The leather belt slashes my backside.

Confused, hurting, and shattered inside, I cry in earnest. Too bullied and intimidated to speak aloud, I silently whisper to myself: *I'm sorry, Daddy! I'm sorry I don't know how to play. I didn't mean to be bad.*

Crack!

"Daddy, please stop!"

Crack!

Crack!

This memory of Dad's "game" is so vivid I find myself rubbing my face, trying to wipe away that nasty slobber. It doesn't do any good. Neither time nor soap nor water can wash Dad's spit from my face. It has left my soul stained and clings tightly to my face like a mask of shame.

More than once Dad screams as he beats me: "I've created a monster! You're no good! You're going to die in a gutter!"

What makes me a monster? Why am I so bad that I need to die in a gutter?

The pain of the physical beatings is swallowed up in the deeper pain of those hateful words. My father's words pierce deep into my soul and shatter my core. I crave Dad's approval, but instead he despises me and relishes telling me so.

* * * * *

When I'm around ten years old, Dad catches me lying and orders me to come into the kitchen. He grabs a large meat cleaver and shouts, "I'm going to cut off your fingers! Lay your hand on the table!"

Staring into his furious eyes, I realize he's capable of mutilating me. Terror sweeps over me. My emotions go haywire as I beg him to please stop!

Dad becomes a snarling beast, screaming even louder for me to lay my hand on the table. I'm afraid to disobey him but can't force myself to place my hand on the table. Every emotion in me screams at once, but Dad's screams finally out-scream my emotions.

My body feels like water as I numb my emotions, shakily place my hand on the table, close my eyes, and wait . . .

Thud!

This is no dull thud; it's a massive, jarring THUD!

I open my eyes, expecting to see my severed fingers in a pool of blood. Instead, the blade has gashed the table next to my hand. Without a word, Dad turns and leaves the room.

*　*　*　*　*

During another episode, Dad finishes beating me with his cane, then drops it to the floor, panting from exhaustion.

"Get out!" he yells.

Believing I'm leaving home for good, I leave the house and walk the Chicago streets alone all evening. I think: *Now I'm on my own, and I'll have to find a place to live,* so I wander into a gas station.

> My soul is so damaged and bruised that Dad's rare expressions of kindness can't reach my open wounds.

"Sir," I say to the attendant, "do you know where I can find a place to live?"

"Sure," he says kindly. "Just go inside and sit down."

He calls the police, who bring me home. Dad's rage has passed, and he cries, hugs me, and apologizes.

"I never thought you would take me seriously and leave," he says.

I'm relieved I can sleep in my own bed on this night, but his hug and apology don't reach as deep as the pain of what he has done to me. My soul is so damaged and bruised that Dad's rare expressions of kindness can't reach my open wounds.

Dad is so sure I'm a disgusting monster and worthless piece of garbage that I believe he's right. I'm a hopeless failure, a loathsome tumor on the earth who nauseates the world simply because I exist.

How can I make myself worth loving? What must I change so my mom won't want to kill herself and leave us? How can I make my dad accept me?

Chapter 4

"COIN, YOU'RE A DUD"

I slowly shuffle toward home from school, in no hurry to get home. Not that school is better than home; I face the same rejection there too. I'm obese and not athletic, and I dread playground games that involve choosing teams. The captains choose me last, letting me know I'm not welcome on their team. My thoughts fall into a familiar pattern: *What's wrong with me? Why don't they want me?*

I'm puzzling over this dilemma when I lift my eyes and see a big red ambulance parked in front of our house. Mom is lying motionless and unresponsive on the stretcher the medics are rolling out to the ambulance.

No one appears to notice me as I silently watch the paramedics load Mom into the back of the ambulance and drive away. I climb the steps and enter our house. Once again, I'm trying to understand why Mom wants to take her life.

I find no answers. When Mom comes home from the hospital, nothing has changed. Dad mocks her because she's too incompetent to kill herself, and she lashes out at him in desperate fury. On two more occasions I watch Dad rush Mom to the hospital after she slits her wrists.

* * * * *

Hebrew school is one of my escapes from our crazy home. Although my parents are ethnically Jewish, they don't practice Judaism at home. However, they want me to become a good Jew, so they send me to Hebrew school two or three afternoons a week and to Shabbat services on Saturday.

Learning our beautiful Hebrew language gives me pride and satisfaction that I'm participating in something God-sized. It connects me with a big God, one I want to believe in. However, as I learn more about our people, I discover that for centuries Jews have been hated by the world around us.

Is that why nobody likes me? I wonder. *Because I'm a Jew? But Dad's a Jew too, so why would he hate me for being one?*

> Learning our beautiful Hebrew language gives me pride and satisfaction that I'm participating in something God-sized. It connects me with a big God, one I want to believe in.

Although I can't make sense of people's hatred for Jews, I feel it all around me. It's less here in a Jewish neighborhood, but we've moved around a lot. When we live in poor, gang-infested areas of Chicago, I feel hatred from other ethnic groups. Instead of feeling compassion for the six million Jews killed during the recent Holocaust, many Americans resent and blame us for causing World War II. After all, some of their sons, brothers, and husbands recently died while fighting to save "those Jews" from Hitler.

A bronze plaque hangs on the wall of our synagogue's foyer; it commemorates the Jews who perished in Hitler's killing frenzy. It reads something like, "Six Million, How Can I Forget?" One Sabbath Day an old man with gnarled fingers and a tired, stooped body pauses in front of the plaque. His body heaves with uncontrollable sobs. *Was this man in a concentration camp? Did he lose loved ones there?* I'm not going to ask, but I wonder if this is how life is supposed to be for us Jews.

Dad spends most of our family's money on Scotch, cigarettes, women, and gambling at the horse track. We always have plenty of junk food in the house: Oreo cookies, Twinkies, Hostess cupcakes. We eat lots of fast food: McDonald's hamburgers, drippy French fries, pizza. We rarely drink water or milk; it's usually Kool-Aid or soda pop. Dad allots Mom twenty dollars per week for groceries. She clips coupons and hops from store to store for the best deals.

Because my parents believe we can't afford clothes, when school gets out for the summer I go barefoot, wearing only short pants and a white T-shirt or no shirt. Just before school starts, Grandpa Jim takes me to a clothing warehouse owned by his Jewish friend, and Grandpa Jim buys me all the shirts and pants I'll need for the coming year.

* * * * *

When I'm around 11, Dad's airline job moves us to Atlanta. I've made my first real friends here in this Jewish neighborhood in Chicago, and I don't want to leave them. How can I move away from Uncle Bert and Aunt Audrey? They're the only adults who love me, and the only ones I trust. Furthermore, there's Sarah, my new sweetheart, and my young heart believes we're in love. I don't want to move, but no one disagrees with Dad when his mind is made up.

As we drive away from our house on Hamlin Avenue to start a new life in Georgia, I'm sitting alone in the back seat. Looking back at the house we're leaving, I can't hold back tears. Although our house has been the scene of unspeakable childhood horrors, it has offered a sense of stability and permanence in my chaotic world. I believe my childhood is over, and now I'm entering the dark, ugly, smelly world of adulthood.

When we settle into our Atlanta apartment, I quickly discover that hatred and discrimination are worse in Atlanta than in Chicago. Atlanta in 1960 is a stronghold of racial prejudice and Jim Crow laws, and the locals view Jews and blacks with equal contempt. They also despise Yankees, and as a Yankee Jew I'm automatically an outcast. Because I'm from Chicago, my classmates call me Al Capone.

> As a Yankee Jew I'm automatically an outcast. Because I'm from Chicago, my classmates call me Al Capone.

At first, I'm amused at how Southerners pronounce my name. Cohen becomes "Coin" in their Southern drawl. One day my Georgia History teacher stands in front of the class, looks straight at me, and says, "Coin, you're a dud! Do you know what a dud is? It's a firecracker that fizzles when you light the fuse. And that's what you are—a dud!"

While the class roars with laughter and my heart numbs, I keep my face blank. After all, I'm supposed to be hated by "normal" people. Why should I expect anything else?

I start hanging out with Mike, a boy my age with a single mom. Like me, he tries to stay out of his house. Without a dad at home, Mike doesn't get beatings like I do, but our homes are similar in other ways.

Mike soon teaches me to shoplift. I've been stealing from my parents since early childhood. Mom and Dad keep pennies in an old giant whiskey bottle and quarters in a quart jar. When the bottle and jar are full of coins, I'll skim a few off. I also rummage through Mom's purse and count the dollar bills. If I think there's enough, I peel one off for myself.

I use the stolen money to purchase snacks and toys. When Mom and Dad ask where I got the new toy, I claim a friend gave it to me or that I found it. Maybe Dad suspects what I'm doing, but he never probes any deeper.

I also steal Dad's whiskey. He marks the liquor level in his bottle with a piece of tape. Whenever I take a swig from the bottle, I add water to bring the level back even with the tape.

* * * * *

One day Mike shows me a duffel bag he stole from Sears. He pulls out a .22 caliber pistol he's shoplifted, just for thrills. Mike and I return to Sears and steal a leather holster and several boxes of bullets. What a rush! Then we steal pens, pencils, transistor radios, and other small items from dime stores.

I still miss Chicago, and especially my sweetheart Sarah. After we move to Atlanta, I call her collect several times, and we awkwardly chat and listen to each other breathe for hours at a time. I trust her because she's one of the few people who hasn't rejected me. I'm 12 and she's 13—I imagine our puppy love is a great romance—and I long to be with her.

When I tell Mike how great Chicago is, he suggests we run away from home. So one Friday we grab our duffel bag with the pistol and bullets and hop on a passenger train headed for Chicago. By mingling with the crowd on the station platform, Mike and I sneak onto a northbound train without tickets.

"When the train starts moving, head for the bathroom," Mike explains. "After the conductor has checked everyone's tickets, we'll come out. Whenever we're not hiding in the bathroom, we'll split up to avoid attracting attention. If anyone questions you, say you're traveling to Chicago with your parents and they're in the other car."

We slip into the nearest bathroom. All night we somehow avoid the porter. Sometimes we sit in the train car, but whenever we approach a station, we hide in the bathroom again. We know the porter locks the bathrooms right before the train reaches the station, so as the train slows for a stop, we hide inside but don't lock the door. Since the door's unlocked, the porter assumes the bathroom's empty and locks it from the outside. Once the train rolls northward again and the porter has checked tickets, he unlocks the door, and we repeat the cycle.

Here we are, two 12-year-old boys, riding a night train, alone from Atlanta to Chicago. We arrive in Chicago early Saturday morning, still undetected by the railroad staff. We find a payphone outside the station, and I call my girlfriend.

"Hey Sarah, it's Phil!" I say, feeling refreshed by the cool morning air on my skin.

Before I can tell her I'm in Chicago, Sarah says, "I don't want to see you."

"Why?" I ask, devastated. The click is my only answer. It's clear she's done with me. Years later I'll find out my collect calls left her parents with a phone bill of several hundred dollars, and they probably forbade her to talk with me.

"No problem!" I bluff, not wanting Mike to know I'm shattered by this newest rejection. "We'll find my friends Larry and Morris."

We board a city bus to the Northside neighborhood I remember so well.

"Phil! I thought you moved to Atlanta," Larry says when he opens the door. Morris peers over his shoulder, looking equally surprised.

"I did move, but I came back on the train," I crow. "This is my friend Mike. He came with me, and look!" I open the duffel bag and pull out the pistol, neatly tucked into the leather holster. Just as I had imagined, my friends' eyes widen in wonder.

"Wow! Can I see it?" Larry asks.

"Be careful. It's loaded," I say, feeling important. "And how about this?" I hold up a box of ammo.

"Let's put this away," Larry says, nervously handing me the pistol. "This gun could get us into big trouble."

"Not us," Mike sneers, his lips curling like a tough guy. "We knew better than to show it off in Atlanta, but this is Chicago. We're gangsters now!"

He removes the pistol from its holster, aims at a nearby mailbox, and pulls the trigger. *Pow! Pow!* Two small holes pop into the mailbox.

I turn triumphantly to Larry and Morris, expecting admiration and respect. Instead, they become morbidly silent.

"Hey," Morris says suddenly. "Let's show my uncle Grover and see what he thinks."

A short time later, I'm watching Grover examine the pistol, turning it over and over in his hands.

"Nice gun," he says at last. "But if the police pick you up and find this gun, you kids are in serious trouble."

His expression darkens, and he continues. "I understand this stuff. I just got out of prison." He pauses, fumbles for his wallet. "Hey, boys, here's twenty bucks. Get some supper and go see a movie. I'll keep your gun, and when you come back, I'll help you figure out how to get home."

I'm ready to protest, but Mike says, "Sure. We'll be back in a few hours."

"He's crazy," Mike says to me as soon as we get away from Grover and my two friends.

"You shouldn't have given him that pistol. It's gone now," I snap at Mike.

"Yeah, but we don't have to worry about getting caught with a stolen gun," Mike explains.

"I'll tell you one thing, Mike. I'm not coming back here so he can 'help' me go home. I'm never going back to more of my dad's beatings."

We wander the Chicago streets for hours. Finally, around midnight, we're standing on a train station platform in one of the roughest neighborhoods in Chicago. As we ponder our next move, a policeman approaches us.

"Where you boys headed?" he asks.

I glance at the sign over the platform and take a cue. "New Orleans," I say as smoothly as I can.

"You boys come with me," says the cop in a no-nonsense tone.

My shoulders slump in weary resignation as we follow him into his cramped little office.

"Where are your parents?" the officer demands as he sinks into a chair behind the desk.

"They're waiting for us in New Orleans," Mike says. His tone, though, is anything but convincing.

"C'mon kids, don't give me that!" The policeman leans across the desk, staring straight at us. "What are you doing in the Cottage Grove train station at midnight on a Saturday? Tell me the truth!" Now he's raising his voice.

"It's true," I insist. "My parents just moved from Chicago to New Orleans, and they're expecting us."

"I don't buy that story," the officer snaps. "Tell me the truth. Did you run away from home?"

My head drops in defeat. It's the same helpless feeling I get when Dad's about to beat me. Clearly, we're not bluffing our way out of this.

Bit by bit, the officer drags the truth from us. He finds the holster and bullets in the duffel bag but doesn't ask about a gun. He's more interested in getting our parents' names and sending us home.

* * * * *

Now it's Sunday, and we're sitting on a plane headed for Atlanta. Big Jim, an airline employee and Dad's former coworker, accompanies us to make sure we don't run away again. I'm relieved when Big Jim takes me from the airport to our house. Maybe Dad won't beat me in front of an old friend.

Dad's crying when he opens the door. He bear-hugs me and holds me for a long time. He reeks from alcohol, sweat, and tobacco, and I'm glad that this time the booze has calmed him. His stubbled cheek rubs against mine as he chokes back tears and murmurs my name brokenly.

After several hours, Big Jim leaves. My insides knot in apprehension, but Dad doesn't make any moves to beat me.

The next day, Monday, Mike and I are back in school. The assistant principal summons us to his office. "Everyone in school was looking for you over the weekend. Your parents were worried to death. Where in the world were you two?"

We tell him about our train ride to Chicago and our flight back home. The principal shakes his head and tries to look grave, but his eyes twinkle.

"Well, at least you didn't miss any school," he says at last. "I can't believe you pulled that off between Friday and Sunday."

Reassured by his gentle response, I leave the principal's office with a sigh of relief. *Nobody knows about the gun,* I'm thinking. *I got away with that one.*

I couldn't be more wrong.

Chapter 5

BAR MITZVAH, BARELY

After my weekend adventure in Chicago with Mike, life settles back into a routine. While it's not exactly comfortable, at least it's familiar. Between attending school, roaming the streets, and preparing for my Bar Mitzvah, I'm avoiding home as much as possible.

Although my parents aren't religious, my Bar Mitzvah is a big deal for them—and me. It's supposed to mark my official passage into manhood, and I'm diligently preparing for the big day. My visits to Mrs. Lerner, my Hebrew tutor, provide peaceful respites to my chaotic life. Her old apartment, with its lingering smell of boiled cabbage, is a welcome sanctuary.

"Becoming a man is a once-in-a-lifetime event," Mrs. Lerner reminds me. "When you stand in the synagogue, you must chant your *haphtarah* with dignity, confidence, and assurance."

I nod, eager to prove I'm ready to become a Jewish man. My assigned Torah portion is from 1 Kings 1, when King David is old and nearing the end of his life. He lies in his bed, shivering and cold. No matter how many blankets his servants pile on him, David can't get warm. In desperation, his staff searches the kingdom for a beautiful young virgin who will lie in bed with the king to keep him warm. They find Abishag, and she gets into bed with David to warm him, but David's not interested in sex with her.

* * * * *

As the date of my Bar Mitzvah gets closer, I hear an announcement on the school's PA system.

"We need your help finding a duffel bag that went missing from the gym," the voice says. "It has the student's gym clothes, wallet, and braces. If you know anything about this, please report it to your teacher or the principal."

Who would be dumb enough to steal someone's braces? I think. *Not me, that's for sure.*

Unfortunately, I've been freely bragging about all the stuff Mike and I have been stealing. When the cops start investigating, my fellow students naturally tell their teachers about Mike and me.

One day I arrive home from school to find three men in dark suits sitting in the living room with my parents. I immediately sense trouble.

"Phillip, sit down," Dad says, his tone confirming my fear.

One of the men shows me a badge as he asks, "How old are you, Phillip?"

"Thirteen," I say, swallowing hard.

"We believe you've been involved in stealing," the detective says, staring into my eyes. "When we interviewed students about the stolen gym bag, several of them told us you bragged to them about stealing a pistol, holster, and ammunition."

The air in the room feels suffocating as his words settle on me.

"I didn't steal the duffel bag from the gym," I protest—but I can't look anyone in the eye while defending myself.

"But you have been stealing other things." The detective is making a statement, not asking a question.

"Yes," I whisper, my voice choking in my throat.

"We have to arrest you, Phillip," the man says.

Mom sits in stony silence, but Dad speaks up, his voice tinged with desperation. "My son's Bar Mitzvah is in three days," he protests. "We've already hired the caterers and a band. The photographer is lined up. This will be my son's big day!"

I hardly believe my ears. *Does Dad really care about me?* Is he stepping up to defend me? The momentary feeling of acceptance is as welcome as it is unfamiliar.

"I'm sorry, sir," the detective replies. "We still have to do our job."

"Our relatives have already bought plane tickets!" Dad persists. "We can't have the ceremony without my son. How will that make me look to our family and friends?"

The warmth and acceptance I'm feeling fades as I realize Dad's not concerned about me. He's worried about his reputation if I'm in jail and miss my Bar Mitzvah.

The detectives ignore Dad's protests and escort me to the Fulton County Juvenile Detention Center. The facility feels cold and sterile, like a hospital. When the heavy steel door clangs shut behind me, I look around my cell. The walls are porcelain tile, and the ceiling is institutional white tile. At eye level is a narrow slit in the gray door, and the room has one barred window overlooking a highway exit ramp.

I settle down and spend hours staring out the window, counting how many Volkswagens drive past. The staff treat me well, and I'm relieved to be out of Dad's reach. Even though I'm locked up, my cell feels strangely peaceful; I'm in no hurry to leave.

After two nights, a guard comes in the morning, unlocks the door, and motions me to follow him.

"C'mon, Sonny," he says. "You're going home. I don't know how your dad pulled it off, but he persuaded the judge to let you go."

I follow the guard to the processing area where my dad waits to meet me and take me home.

* * * * *

On Saturday morning I stand behind the synagogue's podium and face an audience of about two hundred. My brand-new navy-blue suit is adorned with a carnation pinned to the lapel and my beautiful silk tallis is draped over my shoulders. On my head I wear a white satin yarmulke with gold embroidery as I chant my Hebrew passage in strong, flowing tones. Mrs. Lerner helped me write a speech about my passage, and I read about the dying king and the lovely young virgin who kept him warm.

As I chant my Hebrew portion and speak, my relatives and parents' friends grow misty-eyed. Dad smiles broadly and wipes an occasional tear from his cheek. As the ceremony continues, he stands straight and tall, his face glowing with pride.

Although my parents are trying to keep my arrest a secret, I think most everyone at my Bar Mitzvah knows. The rabbi delivers a sermon on mercy, and I'm sure more than one person knows how appropriate that is for my situation.

> The rabbi delivers a sermon on mercy, and I'm sure more than one person knows how appropriate that is for my situation.

Despite the quick transition from jail cell to synagogue, the Bar Mitzvah is not an empty ritual. It feels deeply meaningful to me. Now I want more than ever to be a good Jew. I want to wear the tallis and phylacteries and keep kosher. I want to live by Judaism's creeds. Now that I'm a man, I believe a new world of possibilities opens for me to live as I please. And I deeply hope Dad recognizes me as a man and treats me like one.

After the ceremony we celebrate with a live band, dancing, an array of rich foods, and Mogen David wine. As I gaze around at the festivities, I feel both relieved and a little frightened at how close I came to missing all of this.

* * * * *

When I appear in juvenile court on the shoplifting charges, the judge puts me on probation. My probation officer recommends I find a hobby, so I start collecting coins. I buy the blue collector's cards with round holes to insert the coins. The holes are labeled by date and production mint. The goal is to find a coin to fit each hole until the card is filled.

As my collection grows, I learn which coins are rare and most coveted by collectors. My collection includes a few valuable coins, like old Liberty quarters and Indian head nickels. But I never find the grand prize: the 1909 S VDB Lincoln penny.

Mike takes up the same hobby, and soon he tells me, "Hey, I figured out how to steal coins from the coin store. I have a key that opens their display case. One of us needs to distract the owner while the other opens the case on the opposite side of the store and grabs a handful of coins."

Now Mike and I are stealing coins. Wow, a new rush! Our strategy works several times, and we get away with some coins. Then our neighbor Ricky hears what we're doing and wants to join us.

"Don't ever try this alone," I warn Ricky. "It takes two people to pull it off—one to distract the owner and the other to unlock the case and grab the coins."

Ricky doesn't listen. He gets caught when he tries pulling off a heist on his own. Under police interrogation, he admits everything and squeals on Mike and me. For the second time, plainclothes detectives show up at our house and haul me to the juvenile detention center. They lock Ricky, Mike, and me in separate cells.

* * * * *

Once again, I'm enjoying the peace and quiet of jail with no desire to go home. On the third day, the jailer comes and tells me Dad is waiting to take me home.

"I'm not leaving," I tell him.

"I have to release you," he insists, so I reluctantly follow him through a maze of halls where Dad's waiting for me.

The jailer pulls some papers from a file and asks, "What's your name?"

With lips pinched together, I stare into space, refusing to answer.

"C'mon, kid, tell me your name!" the jailer snaps.

"None of your f*&!% business!" I hiss, refusing to look at Dad and giving the jailer my coldest stare.

"Then you're staying here, Sonny Boy," snarls the jailer as he grabs the front of my shirt and slams me against the wall.

I resent his rough treatment, yet there's no way I'm going home. So with no protest from me, he escorts me to a solitary confinement cell. It's a dark room, about twelve feet square, with a blanket on the floor instead of a cot, and a large tin can for a toilet. Only a thin sliver of light comes through the narrow slit in the door.

Alone in the dimly lit cell, I start pacing the perimeter, trying to outrun my own dark thoughts. *Is this the first step toward dying in a gutter like Dad says I will? Will I be in and out of prison for the rest of my life?* I'm 13 years old, and I've convinced myself my destiny is fixed. I walk faster and faster. Finally, I break into a run and continue until I'm exhausted. I place the blanket on the hard floor and drop off to sleep.

＊ ＊ ＊ ＊ ＊

Two days later, Dad shows up. The jailer comes and gets me, doesn't ask my name, and sends me home with Dad.

Chapter 6

DOWNWARD SPIRAL

It's 1966, and I'm in my sixteenth year. We move from Atlanta back to Illinois and settle into Stone Park, a Chicago suburb infested by organized crime. Our house is three blocks from one of Al Capone's former headquarters. It's not unusual for neighbors to be found dead in car trunks or riddled with machine gun bullets.

Teenaged gangs are divided by suburbs. I quickly learn which suburbs are our allies and which our rivals. Dave, a friend from Stone Park who drives a pink 1958 Chevy, gets interested in a girl from a nearby suburb, Melrose Park, one of our rivals. One night five or six of us head for Melrose to duke it out. A fight ensues. I cower, but Dave and a couple of others jump into the battle. A few long minutes later, Dave and the other guys emerge with bloody faces and bruises. Dave has a broken wrist.

Another night, we're driving around carrying some contraband fireworks. One of us tosses a lit M-80 firecracker into a passing convertible, top down, with four or five guys in it. They toss the M-80 out before it explodes, then chase us down until we're stopped at a red light. They pull up behind us, jump out, and surround our car, waving baseball bats and tire irons. The light turns green, and we zoom away without any injuries or damage.

Our neighborhood is anti-Semitic. Although most people in this area are churchgoing, professing Christians, they hate Jews. My friends call me Jew boy. One summer day a bigger kid named Paul asks if he can borrow my bicycle. I tell him no. He knocks me off my bike and takes it from me. Later I get it back and go talk with Paul's dad. I tell him what Paul did.

His response: "I'm not going to do anything about it because you're a Jew."

While our neighborhood is wild and crazy, the tension and danger in our home frighten me even more, and I don't know how to escape.

Many of my friends are dropping out of high school, joining the Marines or Army, and fighting in Vietnam. I'm eager to follow them. The Vietnam conflict is killing many young men my age, but I don't care about the danger. In fact, dying on the battlefield sounds like an easy escape from the hell in our home.

Uncle Bert calls one day and offers a different perspective. He fought in the Korean War, and he wants me to do something better with my life.

"Flip, you have a good mind," he tells me. "Anybody can enlist and go fight in Vietnam, but America needs brains more than brawn. Finish high school and consider going to college. If you really want to join the military, enlist in the Air Force. They'll at least provide you with a good education."

Knowing Uncle Bert cares about my heart, I take his advice and determine to finish high school. Home remains a hellhole I want to avoid at all costs. So I get a job at Robert Hall Clothes and work all the hours they'll give me. When I'm not at work I'm hanging out on the streets with my friends. But avoiding our home doesn't cancel what's happening there. Whenever I let myself think about Dad's drunken rages or his fights with Mom, I feel sick all over.

* * * * *

Dad spends a lot of time partying with the younger people from his work, and it's no secret he's had other women in his life. When Mom's parents give Dad a new Ford convertible for his fortieth birthday, he shamelessly uses it to woo women.

One evening when I come home, Dad wants to confide something to me.

"Hey, Phillip!" he says, his voice strangely excited.

"Hey," I say. "Where's Mom?"

"She's working late." Dad has a curious smirk on his face as he continues, "And I'm preparing a surprise for her."

I try to appear indifferent because I've learned to avoid getting pulled into my parents' conflicts, but something about his tone makes my blood chill. I brace myself for what's coming.

"I'm finally doing it," Dad says enthusiastically, running a hand through his wavy hair. "I've been planning this for a long time, and I can't wait to see the look on your mom's face when she finds out." He smiles maliciously.

"What are you doing?" I ask, keeping my voice even.

"I'm divorcing your mother," he says calmly, like it's no big deal. "The attorney is working on the papers. In a few weeks, your mother will get the letter. I want to be here when it arrives so I can see the look on her face."

He chuckles, but his mouth is set in a thin, cruel line.

"You keep this confidential!" Dad warns.

My eyes drop to the floor and my shoulders sag as I surrender once again to a lifetime of Dad's dominance over me. I nod my head wordlessly, blocking it out of my mind so I'm not tempted to let Mom know what's coming.

"Okay, I won't tell," I mutter as I shuffle to my room and close the door. Out of Dad's sight, I collapse on the bed and bury my head in my hands. Helpless rage and self-hatred sweep over me. I feel trapped and suffocated with no way out.

But as I realize *Dad's going to be leaving Mom,* I feel a surge of mixed grief and relief. Maybe if he leaves, life *could* be better.

Later, I imagine myself asking him, "Why are you telling me about your plans to divorce Mom? Why do you have to torment me with your selfish plans? I don't want to know!"

But I know it won't go well if I question Dad's motives. Maybe he's telling me because he's found another chance to wound me, and he knows when he harms Mom he hurts me more deeply than when he attacks me. I've developed a survival instinct of suppressing the memories of all the cruelty I suffer at his hands, but I can't find a way to do that with the way he treats Mom. I carry a deep, angry grudge for all the injustice he's inflicted on her and for his efforts to recruit me to his side of the conflict.

* * * * *

One day while I'm working at the clothing store, Dad calls me.

"Phillip, it's me," Dad says when I pick up the receiver. "She got the letter, and she went off the deep end!"

I don't want to hear about it, but I can't bring myself to hang up the phone.

"She was yelling and screaming, and when she came after me, I told her that's exactly why I was divorcing her," he says, laughing. "She almost fainted on the spot. Her reaction was everything I hoped it would be."

I want to scream at him. I think to myself: *You're a monster who takes pleasure in torturing your wife—my mother! You delight in seeing her crack up in front of your eyes.* How can I speak my true heart to the father I both love and fear so much?

"I'm moving out today," he states. "I'll let you know soon where I am."

* * * * *

Dad moves out, and Mom immerses herself with renewed vigor in her work as a secretary at the International Harvester truck plant a few blocks from our house. Now parenting alone, she somehow rises to the challenge of caring for her children and devotes more effort and attention to our needs. It's like my siblings and I have a real, loving mom!

Shortly after leaving Mom, Dad contacts me to say he's living with a new girlfriend. He invites me to visit them in their apartment about 10 miles from our home. I know I'll regret it, but I still crave my father's attention. Despite a lifetime of pain and abuse, I hold out hope that something is going to change. Since I don't have a driver's license yet, I ride my bike over to visit Dad and Martha.

He introduces me to his new girlfriend with a contrived show of affection. "Martha, this is my oldest son, Phillip. He's my pride and joy!"

Her expression is much like Mom's, cowering under a bully, and yet also inexplicably drawn to him no matter what he does.

As I look at Martha, who's half Dad's age and only three years older than me, the empty feeling inside me grows.

"We're having a great life together, aren't we, sweetheart?" Dad says, slipping his arm around the young woman. She tries to smile, but I recognize the telltale signs of fear and tension on her face. Her expression is much like Mom's, cowering under a bully, and yet also inexplicably drawn to him no matter what he does.

Inside me I feel a familiar despair as I'm listening to Dad bragging about their wonderful life. He asks me about Mom and how she's doing, but I just say, "She's okay." Trying to win me over and get me to loosen up, Dad offers to let me drive Martha's Mustang. I take the keys and head for the shiny red Mustang. I don't know how to drive, and it's a miracle I don't wreck her sports car. Despite the momentary thrill I get from driving her muscle car, I'm still locked inside myself and don't want to talk to Dad.

As I leave their apartment to ride my bike home, Dad follows me down the hall. He has bragged all evening about his wonderful life, but now the happy mask slips from his face.

"Phillip!" he whispers urgently, his eyes frightened and pleading. "I'm in trouble. I borrowed money from the Mafia, and I can't pay them back. Can you help me out?"

Almost mechanically, I promise Dad I'll withdraw all my savings from the bank and lend him the money.

A few days later, I hand Dad an envelope with about seven hundred dollars in it. "Are you sure you're okay with this?" Dad asks, appearing helpless.

"Yes," I quietly say.

"Thanks. I'll pay you back as soon as I can," he promises.

> However, my craving for a father's love is so strong I'm willing to give away my last dollar if that's what it takes to get him to love me.

Even as I nod wordlessly, I know I'll never see the money. I should have known I couldn't buy my father's affection, not even with my entire life savings. However, my craving for a father's love is so strong I'm willing to give away my last dollar if that's what it takes to get him to love me.

* * * * *

Soon afterward, Dad has one of his mental breakdowns and ends up in the hospital. I enter his room, devastated by what I see. He lies curled in a fetal position in the hospital bed, shattered and feeble.

Dad always tries to project an image of strength and control, but this pathetic man now has no power over anything.

"Hi Dad!" I say with forced enthusiasm, but he only emits a long, shuddering sigh.

Inside, I'm weeping for this broken wreck of a man. Life isn't supposed to be this way. Fathers are supposed to be loving, strong, and protective, not pitiful and tormented like my dad.

"Ask your mother to come," he says hoarsely.

I suppress a scream, thinking, *Why? You treated her like dirt and left her! She doesn't owe you anything! Why should she come to you now?*

But I simply say, "Okay, I'll tell her."

When Mom visits him in the hospital, Dad begs her to take him back. Against all logic, she agrees. When the hospital releases him, he moves back home, and they cancel the divorce.

* * * * *

Martha is pregnant with Dad's child, so Mom and Dad scrape together enough money to pay her off if she agrees to disappear. I'm soon to have a half-sibling. Perhaps there are, or will be, more.

After returning home, Dad spirals deeper and deeper into depression. Now a thick, eerie silence greets me at home. It's a little better than the noise of drunken fighting, but it doesn't last. Soon my parents are fighting as always, and life is crazy and chaotic once again.

Uncle Bert's love and acceptance comes closest to satisfying my longing for a father's love, but he hasn't been well lately.

My job at the clothing store provides an escape, and I enjoy fun times with my coworkers. Our bosses are kindhearted, and I spend as much time as possible there to avoid going home. One day while I'm at work, Mom calls me.

"Uncle Bert had surgery today," she tells me. "When the doctors opened him up, he was so full of cancer they sewed him shut again without doing anything."

I reel in disbelief at the harsh finality of her words. We've all known something's been wrong with my uncle, but I'm not prepared for this.

"He has Hodgkin's disease," Mom continues. "It's incurable. They don't know if he'll live a few months or a few years."

Her words pierce my heart like darts as I see Uncle Bert in my mind. He's kind, funny, loving, caring . . . and now he's dying? Am I going to lose my life's only anchor?

> Her words pierce my heart like darts as I see Uncle Bert in my mind. He's kind, funny, loving, caring . . . and now he's dying? Am I going to lose my life's only anchor?

Numbly, I hang up the phone and grapple with the black monster of despair. Overcome by sorrow, I trudge numbly to the stock room. Sitting down at an old card table, I drop my head into my hands and weep hot, bitter tears of raw anguish.

Mr. Baldi, the manager, comes into the stockroom, but I can't control my weeping. He walks over to me, lays a gentle hand on my shoulder, and stands silently for a few moments.

"I'm so sorry," he says at last.

I'm overcome by his kindness, and I want to turn and weep in his arms, but I hold back. Men don't do that. Still, I'm strangely comforted by my boss's simple gesture of sympathy and caring. He can't possibly guess how desperately my bruised soul yearns for love, but his kind act provides a rare, sweet comfort to my troubled heart.

In the 1960s, doctors allow family members to decide how much to tell the patient about his or her condition, and Aunt Audrey doesn't want Uncle Bert to know he has cancer and is dying. She wants his last days to be happy, so we're warned not to tell him about the cancer.

Still, Uncle Bert senses the truth and sometimes says, "I know I'm dying from cancer."

"You don't know what you're talking about!" Dad scolds.

"Stop talking like that," Mom chimes in. "You're healthy, and you're going to live a long, happy life."

How can I possibly join this grim charade? Whenever I'm with Uncle Bert, I feel Death stalking him, waiting for an opportunity to pounce. But we pretend everything and everyone is fine. We play Password and, as usual, Uncle Bert and I win. However, we're living in a make-believe world where the most important things are stuffed away—out of sight and ignored. I hate the lies and pretense and long for reality, but that means facing the truth about Uncle Bert's condition.

I'm going to lose the only person who loves me unconditionally, but we all engage in an absurd conspiracy to pretend he's doing fine. The tentacles of dark despair wrap around my heart, squeezing ever more tightly.

Chapter 7

MEXICO

In 1967, I graduate from high school near the bottom of my class of about eight hundred seniors. Still desperate to escape our home, I begin the process of enlisting in the Air Force when Dad takes me to Miami for a graduation present. While there, I meet a girl my age from Mexico who tells me about an English-speaking school in Mexico City, the University of the Americas, that might accept me despite my low GPA.

I don't want to attend college. Yet Mexico sounds like an exotic adventure. I'm captivated by the James Bond novels and movies of the '60s, and I crave that flavor of romance and adventure. Since my parents don't want me enlisting in the military and deployed to Vietnam, they like the idea of me going to college, even if it's in Mexico. When my grandfather offers to pay my way, I negotiate a deal that works for everyone.

Only Uncle Bert's illness makes me hesitate. When I tell him good-bye, I can't look him in the eye because he might see the lie I'm living about him. And what if he dies while I'm gone?

When I arrive in Mexico, my worries about Uncle Bert fade into the excitement of this brand-new adventure. I immediately fall in love with the Mexican people and the beautiful Spanish language. In Spanish class I'm an eager student, and after class I wander around the city, practicing Spanish on anyone who'll converse with me. I'm majoring in psychology because I hope it helps me understand messed-up people like me. Like many of us in the '60s, my psychology professors are as crazy as everyone else.

At school I befriend Ed, whose father is an embassy dignitary from an Asian country to Mexico. I hang out with Ed and his well-to-do friends, eating at nice restaurants and drinking Mexican wine. He often invites me to his twenty-six-room mansion, where servants provide us delicious lunches. One night Ed and I meet a hippie-looking guy from California. Somehow the conversation moves toward marijuana. He explains how wonderful it makes you feel.

"Doesn't marijuana lead to hard drugs?" I ask.

"I've never seen it do that," he replies with intense blue eyes framed in long, straight blond hair. The questions and sales pitch continue until Ed and I agree we'll try it once.

Our hippie friend stops his car in a somewhat secluded place facing a park. Ed sits in the back seat while I'm in the passenger seat. Our guide removes an already rolled joint from his wallet, lights it, and explains how to inhale slowly, hold the smoke in, then let it out. He's got smooth music playing over the car radio.

We each inhale the hot smoke while the ember on the end of the joint glows bright red-orange. Then slowly exhale. A pungent, blue-gray cloud fills the car, while a similar cloud fills my head.

The weed transports me into another world. Colors around me are more vivid, and the music swirls with hues and tones I've never experienced before.

I don't like this feeling.

"How long does this stuff last?" I ask our gentle friend.

"Maybe an hour or two," he says dreamily.

The next day Ed and I vow we'll never, never, never smoke weed again.

A week or so later, I'm telling my college roommates about my bad drug experience. They listen intently and sympathetically.

A couple of nights later, the guys are all sitting on the porch. I join their circle. They're passing a joint around. Without a word, the guy next to me hands me the skinny football-shaped wrinkled white paper with a dark gray ribbon of smoke rising from the glowing ash.

Without a word, I take a hit . . .

* * * * *

Mexico City's elevation is around 7,000 feet above sea level, and it's surrounded by a 10,000-foot mountain rim. The city's smog settles into the bowl created by the surrounding mountains, and the air hangs heavy with smog and grit. I leave for school in the morning, freshly showered and wearing clean clothes. By the time classes are finished in the afternoon, my face is greasy, and my collar lined with dark soot. We take two showers a day to stay clean.

In addition to the polluted air, my friends and I daily smoke marijuana and cheap cigarettes. We're getting frequent lung infections and open sores on our bodies that won't heal. When we're feeling sickly and run down, we travel to the coastal village of Pie de la Cuesta, a few kilometers north of Acapulco. The fresh air, sunshine, and saltwater of the Pacific Ocean soon heal our sores.

One of my friends owns a Volkswagen Beetle, and like true hippies, we fit twelve college students into its limited space. Four cram into the front seat, four in the back, and four sit on the sunroof with feet dangling into the car's passenger compartment. We careen around hairpin mountain curves while stoned on marijuana and drunk on tequila and cheap wine. The dangerous roads have no guardrails, and drivers pass one another on blind curves. Somehow, we avoid a deadly accident and make it through alive. It's crazy and stupid, but that's how we're doing life in the 1960s.

Since I've always lived in big cities like Chicago and Atlanta, I perceive the countryside as the dark, spooky corridor between cities. Of course, the cities have plenty of crime and danger, but at least they feel familiar. The open country, to me, is unknown and frightening.

Since I've always lived in big cities like Chicago and Atlanta, I perceive the countryside as the dark, spooky corridor between cities. The open country, to me, is unknown and frightening.

However, in rural Mexico I see something different. I see endless miles of pure, majestic nature. The fluffy white clouds floating in brilliant blue skies and towering mountains take my breath away.

What strikes me even more than the scenery is the people. Many of them are obviously poor, living in bare simplicity, probably unaware of their poverty. Their homes are smaller and more basic than anything I've seen in the worst slums of Chicago. And yet, despite their poverty, these people appear glowing and serene. Whenever I make eye contact with them, most of them respond with broad smiles and waves.

In my Chicago world, money is everything. Life in Chicago is all about greed. My parents fight over money. Money causes betrayals, broken families, robberies, murders. Everyone desperately finds ways to accumulate more money, and I assume that's the way life is supposed to be for everyone. But here in Mexico, I see poor people who appear far happier than anyone I've ever known.

What's their secret?

This mystery haunts me during our weekend trips to Pie de la Cuesta. We stay in a seedy, 50-cents-per-night hotel and hang out on the beach all day. The hotel owners have German shepherds that join us on the beach. We toss coconut shells into the surf, and the dogs happily fetch them; sometimes the dogs join us in body surfing the waves.

Although I can't explain what's happening in me, my heart has cracked open enough to see a new and better world. I want to remain in Mexico forever. That means becoming fluent in Spanish—I know I can do that—and I'm growing to love the romantically melodic tones and meanings of the Spanish language more than the hard, precise Germanic English language.

For example, when you tell your wife, *"Mi amor, mi amor eres tu,"* it plays sweet heartstrings you don't hear when you simply say, "I love you."

Because I'm feeling heart-connected with the Mexican people, I mingle among them and practice my Spanish whenever I can. My language skills improve rapidly until I'm at the top of my Spanish class. My life has, somehow, become a dream.

And then, during a phone call to Dad, I make a huge mistake. I mention those weekend trips to Acapulco.

"Acapulco!" he rages. "That's a resort! That's got nothing to do with your education. You're wasting your grandfather's money. You're not getting any more!"

So the money stops coming. During my last few months in Mexico, I sleep on friends' couches. Although street food is cheap, my money is almost gone. So I steal food from my friends' refrigerators and bread from a local bakery.

Then I get pneumonia. The campus doctor prescribes antibiotics which will take most of my remaining money. I must choose between medicine and food. I choose medicine and lose around forty pounds in my final two to three months in Mexico.

I'm in a desperate place. I want to stay in Mexico and immerse myself in the simple joy I've felt and seen, especially in the rural areas. But I can't find a realistic way to stay. My only option is the one I dread most—returning home.

I want to visit the Pie de la Cuesta beach one last time. So I book my return plane ticket to the U.S. from Acapulco instead of Mexico City. I'm hoping to experience, one more time, that peace and joy I've experienced whenever I've been here, absorbing the hearts of the simple people and the vast majesty of the Pacific Ocean.

The beach is as beautiful and tranquil as ever, and I experience some enjoyment from that final visit. But then, as I'm riding a city bus in Acapulco, someone picks my pocket. The thief gets away with my passport, plane ticket, and few remaining pesos.

The night before my scheduled flight, I arrive at the airport hoping to find someone who can help me. Security is quite lax in the 1960s, and the Mexican officials provide me a temporary ID and let me board my flight home.

* * * * *

Dad meets me at the airport in Chicago, and I can see he's in a foul mood.

"You look terrible!" he says by way of greeting. "Why are you so skinny?"

"I've been sick," I say weakly. "I had to use my last money to buy medicine, and I haven't had much to eat."

Unconcerned about my poor health, Dad shakes his head in disgust. "How come you let your hair grow so long?" he demands. "You look like a bum."

I shrug wordlessly and push my long hair out of my eyes. *Welcome back to the United States,* I think sarcastically. *Welcome back to Chicago. Welcome back to the same old, same old. Welcome home.*

"You're getting a haircut first thing," Dad says, marching me to the airport barber shop. "You're in trouble, Phillip. You've wasted your grandfather's money on booze and parties and who knows what else."

Like you, Dad, I think in my heart.

Feeling old and tired, I settle into the barber's chair. That glimpse of a better life evaporates like a faraway mirage.

Snip . . . snip . . . snip . . . My hopes, my sweet memories, all are falling together to the barber's floor along with my brown locks.

"Cut it short!" Dad orders curtly.

The barber also expresses disgust for me as he jerks my head around. Echoing Dad, he asks, "What kind of trouble did you get yourself into in Mexico?"

"You still look terrible," Dad says after I've been shorn. He wrinkles his nose and adds, "And you stink."

I cast a miserable glance at my reflection in the barber's mirror. All the happiness I had found in Mexico is gone. The familiar feelings of despair wash over me. Quoting Simon and Garfunkel, I mumble, "Hello, darkness, my old friend."

As we leave the barber shop, I make a last-ditch effort to get back to the only real happiness I've ever known.

"Dad, I want to go back to Mexico. It was beautiful there. I loved the people. I belong there."

"Absolutely not!" Dad explodes, and I know it's useless to argue. My brief illusions of happiness, peace, and purpose are gone. I'm back in my personal hell, and it's about to get worse.

When we arrive home from the airport, Mom tells me, "Uncle Bert is going down fast. He could die anytime."

The next day, I'm headed to visit my uncle in the hospital.

"Don't stay too long," Mom warns me before I leave the house. "And if Bert asks how he looks, tell him he's getting better. Don't even hint that he's dying."

I enter the hospital room and stare quietly at my beloved uncle. His face is turned away from me as he stares blankly at the wall. I thought my time in Mexico had left me skinny, but Uncle Bert is a living skeleton draped in yellow skin. One of his legs is black and blue and swollen to a grotesque size.

I study him for a few moments before he notices I'm there. Uncle Bert slowly turns his head toward me. Strong pain medicine has fogged his brain, but eventually he recognizes me. A weak smile crosses his skeletal face.

"Hi, Flip," he slurs. "How are you?"

"I'm okay," I say, fighting back tears.

"How was Mexico?"

"It was good."

"What do you think?" he asks weakly. "Do I look like I'm getting better?"

Nearly choking on the senseless lie, I manage to say, "Yeah, you're looking great."

As his eyes meet mine, I feel him assuring me he understands why I'm lying to him.

We share a long moment of intimate silence.

Now it's time to leave, and we shake hands the way he taught me—firmly and confidently with sincere eye contact. But this time I've got the strong grip while Uncle Bert is even weaker than I had been when he taught me how to shake hands the first time.

"Goodbye, Uncle Bert," I say hoarsely.

"Goodbye, Flip."

With everything in me, I'm holding back the dam inside. I exit the hospital room and close the door behind me. Then the dam breaks. My shoulders shake with sobs as I stumble down the hospital corridor, hating myself for lying to my beloved uncle in his dying moments. I want to die with him. Without him, my life is empty.

Uncle Bert dies the next day, and part of me dies with him. Dreams of Mexico, college, and a better life also fall into a dark, bottomless abyss.

And yet, something inside me has changed. A small flame burns deep inside from what I experienced in Mexico. Something in me says that what I saw was real. Somewhere out there is a better life. If ordinary people have found it, maybe—just maybe—I can find it too.

And though part of me died with Uncle Bert, part of him now lives inside me.

Chapter 8

WALLY

After experiencing Mexico, I'm convinced that life in the United States is about money. People live for it, talk about it, and destroy one another in their endless quests for more. As I fondly think about those poor but contented Mexican people, American materialism nauseates me.

I'm beginning to believe that more money doesn't equal more happiness, but I can't find anyone who agrees with me. I wonder if I'm crazy—truly crazy.

My grandpa dies in 1969, leaving my mom a sizeable inheritance. Around that time, Dad tells us he's quitting his airline job.

"Sixteen years is long enough for one job," he declares. "We're moving to Miami."

Years later, I learn the truth: Dad came to work drunk and got fired.

Unlike our earlier move to Atlanta, I'm good with moving to Miami. Dad's parents live in Miami, and I've always enjoyed visiting the beach-lined, sun-drenched city. Using Mom's inheritance, we purchase a lovely house in a quiet neighborhood. Our new home is surrounded by fruit and palm trees with a swimming pool in the backyard.

Dad finds a job managing a restaurant, a position he enjoys because he can hit on the young waitresses who work for him. He gives me a generous allowance, and I spend it on bell-bottom trousers and madras shirts. One day Dad throws me the keys to a brand-new sports car, a 1969 AMC Rambler Javelin. It's white inside and out with wide tires and halfmoon hubcaps. With my new car and stylish clothes, I have no problem finding girlfriends . . . but I'm still not happy. I long for the peace I experienced in Mexico, the harmony with nature and detachment from material possessions. Although I enjoy the beauty and warmth of south Florida, it doesn't satisfy my tormented mind.

I attend community college, continuing my major in psychology, hoping it will help me understand my inner chaos. It's interesting, but it doesn't address the screaming void in my soul.

"There has to be more to life than this," I tell my parents.

"You're going through a stage," Mom says. "You'll get over it. Finish school, find a job, and get married. That's what life is about."

I stare at the floor, frustrated as I remember the words of a Peter and Gordon song: "I don't care what they say, I won't stay in a world without love."

"If that's all life is about," I tell my parents, "I'd rather be dead."

Despite all the beauty of Miami, I feel trapped in the same inescapable dark bubble that imprisoned me in Chicago. Sometimes I wonder if I imagined my wonderful time in Mexico. Drugs are the only part of my Mexican experience also available in Miami, so I escape into drugs. Getting high offers temporary relief, and that's better than nothing.

* * * * *

The 167th Street beach—right in the middle of the tourist district—is a gathering place for many young kids my age. The beach is crowded with hundreds of hippies, most of us hanging out, getting high, and sipping cheap wine.

I come there whenever I can. One night I'm shuffling along the beach, carrying my shoes and feeling the sand between my toes.

"Hello, my friend, how are you?" I hear a gentle voice with a slight Latino accent.

I look where the voice is coming from, and that's when I meet Wally. Sitting cross-legged on the sand and playing a sitar, Wally carries the air of an Indian guru. His bony fingers dance like butterflies up and down the sitar's long neck while it points at the night sky. The delicate melodies he plucks weave brightly colored threads through my fevered brain.

"The music's talking to you," Wally says, with a steady stare that shoots straight through me. "Can you hear its message?"

I shake my head in frustration while Wally plays. His soulful eyes remain fixed on me as his head gently bobs in time to the music.

"What's it saying?" I ask.

Wally doesn't answer. Lost inside his music, he closes his eyes and continues playing.

* * * * *

I start visiting Wally often at the cheap boarding house room he's renting. He dims the electric lights and lights a single candle and incense, then plays his classical guitar or sitar for hours on end. When he's not playing, he sits in deep silence.

I need a friend, and hanging out with Wally comforts me. I think he understands me. I imitate Wally's clothing, way of speaking, and mannerisms. I buy a cheap guitar and awkwardly try playing like Wally, but compared to his agile fingers and flowing tones, my playing is clumsy and clunky.

Wally's a small-time drug dealer selling heroin and LSD. Since he lives simply and frugally, selling a few drugs pays his bills and leaves many hours free to play music. Wally always offers me a hit of some drug and some deep, spontaneous guitar or sitar playing to release me from the prison of my life.

In addition to music, Wally also writes poetry, which he sometimes recites, holding me spellbound. Wally's steady flow of music, drugs, and poetry transports me into a better world, and I want more.

> Wally's steady flow of music, drugs, and poetry transports me into a better world, and I want more.

* * * * *

On New Year's Eve 1969, I take a huge dose of LSD. Soon my inner world is spinning in endless, spiraling circles. LSD is highly hallucinogenic, amplifying every sensation, thought, and feeling. When those feelings are good, LSD explodes a person into higher euphoric ecstasies. When they're negative, the drug takes you on a bad trip of apocalyptic terror.

I'm in beautiful Miami on New Year's Eve with a new sports car, no girlfriend, and no party to attend. On this night, the LSD plunges me into a turbulent abyss of despair so vast and deep I only think of one way out.

I'm going to kill myself, I think as my drug-fueled mind endlessly replays my meaningless life.

My parents don't care if I live or die. Girls don't want me. Uncle Bert's dead. I have nothing to live for, and I'm tired of living. I'm going to drive my car full speed into a wall.

Wally's my only friend, and I'm going to tell him about my plans to kill myself. Around midnight I park my car in front of his house. While my body walks to Wally's front door, my mind floats in another universe. I'm somewhere outside myself, watching and hearing my knuckles rap on the door.

Bam, bam, bam. The knock sounds like the distant echo of a drum.

"Come in," Wally calls.

I step inside and close the door. A young prostitute sits on the bed, shooting up heroin. She appears worn out. Her head moves in slow motion as she looks up at me.

"Are you hurting, dude?" she asks.

"Yeah," I whisper.

"I understand." Her tired eyes meet mine.

I always thought prostitutes were hardened and cold, but for the first time in my life, even without any physical contact, I feel an emotional connection with someone other than Uncle Bert. It's a strange sensation, and I want more.

When she leaves, I sit down at Wally's old brown card table.

"I'm going to kill myself," I tell him.

"Go ahead," he calmly replies.

Did I hear that right? Surely, I'm tripping and he said something else! My friend cares so little about me that he won't try to talk me out of suicide? He's supposed to say something, to plead with me, to reason with me about how good life is. Instead, he calmly says, "Go ahead."

Go ahead . . . go ahead . . . go ahead . . . Those words ricochet through the swirling, colored, flashing apocalypse the LSD has created inside me.

That's all? Just . . . Go ahead?

"Are you lonely?" Wally asks, breaking the silence.

I stare into empty space, too dumbfounded to breathe.

Am I lonely? I don't know. The words "Are you lonely?" settle into my soul, and every cell in my body cries out from the hell of loneliness. I'm alone, unloved, and unwanted. I'm imprisoned in a world of make-believe and pretense. My life is a fraud. I've got a new sports car, the latest clothes, the drugs, the alcohol, the girls—*it's all fake!*

Although I crave authenticity and reality, my only reality is my desperate loneliness. I want to leave all this pain behind, but won't death also be forever lonely? I don't want to live, and I don't want to die.

"Why don't you write?" Wally asks. He places a pencil and paper on the table.

I stare at the paper, trying to extract something—anything—from the kaleidoscopic images tumbling madly in my brain. I press pencil to paper, make a dot, then erase it. Two or three times I make a new dot, then erase it, rubbing so hard I make the rickety old table jiggle.

Drawing the dot. Erasing the dot. Drawing the dot. Erasing the dot. It soothes me for a moment, but then something snaps. A thunderstorm explodes in my head with blinding flashes of lightning and deafening thunder. The storm inside is trying to blow me apart.

Wally senses my panic and injects Demerol, a strong narcotic, into my veins, assuming it will calm me. Instead, the drug hurls me into a more distant universe as the madness freefalls me into faraway galaxies.

Sitting on the floor with his legs crossed, Wally plucks and strums his guitar. His fingers dance gracefully along the strings, creating delicate, soothing melodies that penetrate my disturbed mind. The sounds wash over me like breakers on the Mexican beach, gradually soothing my inner torment and turbulence.

Like a warm blanket, the melody envelopes me, easing my pain. Momentarily released from my life's madness, I stand still in a hurricane's eye while the debris of my broken life crashes and spins around me. Then a moment of peace as the music embraces me. I've always enjoyed music, but this is the first time I actually *hear* music and *feel* its soul. I feel the musician struggling with pain like mine. The musician's lonely cry fills the notes and the beats, and my soul cries along.

Somewhere in that timeless night, Wally plays his sitar. He sits with the instrument's large gourd anchored firmly in the triangle of his crossed legs while the sitar's neck angles upward toward Heaven.

His long, bony fingers glide up and down the neck, pressing the frets that twang out the thinly threaded notes. Each note bursts into my brain as bright, delicate, and unique as a snowflake. The sound flows in gold and silver threads that weave the notes together in rhythmic, poetic sequences carried deep into my chattering brain.

I'm a prisoner in an artificial world of frills, fun, and masks. Everywhere I look, nothing is real. People are fake. Life is fake. I'm fake. But loneliness is real. It's the only real thing in Miami, where I see wealth and pleasure and beautiful women and liquor and drugs and dazzling lights and broken homes and broken lives and dead people walking around in living bodies.

But the music, the music that's always been here—the soul of the melodies I never heard before—all of that is real. It's healing, and it's good.

Wally asks me another jolting question. He stops playing for a moment, looks serenely at me, and asks, "What's your purpose?"

"My purpose?"

He nods, closes his eyes, and continues playing the sitar from the silence deep inside.

Wally's latest question echoes through the hollow canyons of my soul. *Am I supposed to have a purpose? Do I have a reason to live? Why don't I know my purpose? Why hasn't anyone told me?*

"What's my purpose?" I ask Wally.

He doesn't answer or open his eyes.

Chapter 9

AIMLESS

My experience the night at Wally's house when I planned to kill myself stirs a restless hunger for something. I don't know what it is, but it's consuming me. Wally's questions— "Are you lonely?" and "What's your purpose?"—haunt me constantly. I've got a nagging sense that my purpose includes something called God, but I stifle the thought. I don't want to say or think the word *God*. The Judeo-Christian God represented by the middle-class America of the 1950s and '60s has hurt me to the core.

Feeling restless, I leave home to "find myself," as we call the search for meaning in the 1960s.

Against my parents' wishes, I drop out of college and return to Chicago. Leaving behind the beautiful house and my new sports car, I board a Greyhound bus for the trip north. My grandma has offered me a room in her apartment, and she finds me a job in a factory.

My new job is repetitive and boring; I run a punch press that stamps out lids for dog food cans. Wearing large earmuffs to muffle the machine's loud *THUMP! THUMP! THUMP!*, I'm lost inside my head, with only my turbulent thoughts for companions to the punch press's steady thumping beat. Away from Dad's nagging, my hair is growing long again. Also, because it feels good, I get high whenever I can.

After a few weeks of stamping out dog food can lids, the boss calls me into his office.

"We're hearing about conversations you're having with other workers," he says flatly. "It sounds like you're a communist, so we're letting you go."

"I don't know what you're talking about," I protest. But he's done talking with me.

Now I'm unemployed, but I'm not interested in hunting for another job. Instead, I hang around my grandma's apartment, leaving once or twice a day to go outside and smoke weed.

At first, Grandma offers to help me. "Do you think I could help you start a business?" she asks.

"I can't think of a business I'd want," I say indifferently. "Well, maybe a head shop would be cool." A head shop—of course! That's a store that sells psychedelic posters, black lights, drug paraphernalia, and other items to enhance the experience of getting high.

Grandma doesn't answer, and I'm trying to convert her to my hippie beliefs. I preach about free love and expanding one's consciousness.

"Our capitalist economy is going to fail," I tell her. "Unless you want to lose all your money, you should buy land so you have something left after the crash."

"I can't handle you living here any longer," she says. "I don't agree with your communist beliefs. It's time you move on." Since communism is America's greatest enemy, anyone who challenges the system or thinks differently in any way is labeled a communist.

My hippie views are too far out for my dear old grandmother, and she finally asks me to leave.

"I can't handle you living here any longer," she says. "I don't agree with your communist beliefs. It's time you move on."

Since communism is America's greatest enemy, anyone who challenges the system or thinks differently in any way is labeled a communist.

"I talked with my friend who owns apartments," Grandma tells me. "She said she'll rent you an efficiency apartment near the lake." She's willing to help me even as she sends me on my way. "I'll pay the deposit and the first month's rent. And the landlady knows someone who will give you a job."

* * * * *

Around that time, I meet Jim and John, two wandering hippies from Virginia. They need a place to crash, so I invite them into my apartment. After a few days, John heads back to Virginia while Jim remains with me. Jim is a self-declared poet, so we write poetry together.

"You write a line, I write a line, you write a line, I write a line," he explains.

It's a fascinating new experience, improvising and pooling our creativity. Wally sparked in me a love for the magic of words, and now Jim's fanning that flame.

My new employer is an exclusive hotel popular with celebrities. I'm thinking I'm a cool desk clerk sitting in swanky surroundings. Sorely lacking people skills, I soon get fired from this job too.

When I lose the job, I tell Jim.

"So you lost your job," he says with an indifferent shrug. "Now what?"

"I'm dropping out and joining you. I want to be free. I want to go wherever I want. I'm sick of working a job. My grandma said she'll only help me keep this apartment as long as I'm working, so I'll lose this place. But I don't care."

"That's right," Jim says with his peaceful smile. "We don't need an apartment. We'll live on the road."

I'm good with that because I'm ready to leave Chicago. I thought returning to the Windy City was coming home, but it hasn't done anything for me. I'm still lonely, bored, and restless. When I'm not working, I'm wandering the streets and lakefront, sometimes all night.

"Life gets better," Jim assures me as I pack a few belongings into an old army duffel bag.

We wander into a park where a man sitting on a bench addresses us as we stroll past.

"My brothers," he says in a deep, slow voice, "my name is Tinny."

Tinny is tall and skinny and wears a robe about two sizes too large for his slender frame. He has a long scraggly beard and matted hair that hangs past his shoulders. Although it's difficult to see his features through all that hair, I'm guessing he's in his early thirties.

"Sit," Tinny offers, and we sit next to him, grateful for the chance to rest our bodies. Tinny's eyes twinkle and his bearded cheeks move, so I know he's smiling even though I can't see his mouth. His mustache is matted with dried food.

Jim nudges me uneasily, and I sense he's wondering if this guy is going to rob us.

As if reading our thoughts, Tinny laughs. "My commune is safe. Peace, my brothers," he says, holding up two fingers in the peace sign.

"We are all brothers and sisters," he continues in his deep, calm, reassuring voice. "We have nothing but peace and love. Love is the greatest, and it's offered to all."

To demonstrate his love, he throws his long arm around my shoulder. *Phew!* I catch my breath at the stench of his unwashed body, but I'm so hungry for love I don't care about the smell. When Tinny stands and invites us to his place, Jim and I follow.

His "commune" is an old, small, second-floor apartment. Thin bluish-gray ribbons of smoke rise lazily from incense burning in an ashtray on the coffee table. Bare light bulbs illuminate the sparsely furnished apartment—which is crowded with about twenty people. They're passing around joints, cigarettes, and a wine jug. No one seems to notice us or even be slightly bothered by our arrival.

We spend a couple days in the commune getting to know Tinny and the others.

After a few days Tinny tells Jim and me about a rock music festival in Wisconsin. "It will be a gathering of brothers and sisters," he says. And then, as if conferring a great favor, he adds, "You may accompany me."

Jim and I look at each other and shrug.

"Sure, why not?" we tell Tinny. The crowded apartment is stale and steamy in the summer heat, and it's not the life I want anyway. Getting out of Chicago sounds like a good first step.

* * * * *

Thousands of hippies converge on a farm for that Wisconsin rock festival. Vans, tents, and trucks with canvas tops dot the fields while beer, wine, drugs, and sex flow freely and music fills the air.

Rock bands scream and stomp on the wooden stage. Music is blasting from giant speakers. We sway and stagger to the rhythms and lyrics that don't always make sense. One band after another plays nonstop day and night.

On the evening of the second day, Jim says, "Let's leave. I'm not into this anymore." I agree. We find Tinny and tell him we're leaving.

"Ah, peace, brothers," Tinny says. "Take the car and drop it in Chicago. I'll get a ride back to Chicago when I'm ready."

Jim and I drive back to Chicago, leave the car at Tinny's place, and hitchhike to Ohio, where we sleep in an open field. The next morning, we wander onto the Kent State University campus. A couple of weeks before, National Guardsmen had opened fire on an anti-war demonstration there, killing four students and injuring nine more.

The killings have sent shock waves through the country, and we're becoming bitter toward the police, government, and anyone in authority. Crosby, Stills, Nash, and Young express our pain and rage when they sing,

"Tin soldiers and Nixon coming,
We're finally on our own.
This summer I hear the drumming.
Four dead in Ohio."[2]

Indeed, we believe we're on our own, abandoned by our own country. An overwhelming sadness grips me as we wander through the site of the massacre under the watchful eyes of the police. I can't wait to get away from that eerie place and hitchhike south to Virginia.

Hitchhiking is common in the '60s, and it's easy to thumb rides. Jim and I are only two among thousands of young people drifting around the country, restless and aimless. We protest the Vietnam War and dodge the draft that sent many of our friends into that conflict. Feeling that America and its religions have failed us, we seek enlightenment through drugs, sex, and mystical Eastern religions.

I have four hundred dollars in cash from my final paycheck. Jim and I head to Old Town to score a kilo or two of marijuana. Then we'll divide it up and sell it to make some extra money.

Instead, we're robbed, beaten, and left bloodied.

Most of us hippies are peaceful and generous. We want peace, love, and sharing. We freely share our food, money, cars, drugs, wine, and cigarettes. We're united in a desire for peace in our troubled world.

America is divided into two major factions: those who want the Vietnam War and those who don't. Before going to Mexico, I was a patriotic "greaser" in favor of war and killing. Through the peer pressure I experienced from my fellow students in Mexico, I've become anti-Vietnam, anti-establishment, and against just about everything America stands for.

On our side of the divide, we're experiencing a strange phenomenon. Although we protest the Vietnam War and refuse to fight in that faraway land where young soldiers are lonely, afraid, and homesick, another war rages in our souls. We too are lonely, afraid, and homesick—yet we're not in some faraway trench. Even when surrounded by crowds at a rock festival or a protest, we feel deeply alone.

Chapter 10

NOMAD

After several weeks on the road, Jim heads back to his home in Virginia. I travel to a huge rock music festival near Atlanta. By some accounts, more than three hundred thousand young people are here for three days of nonstop live music, drugs, and free love. Among other acts, Jimi Hendrix splits the midnight air with a thunderous rendition of "The Star-Spangled Banner" on the Fourth of July. He plays to the backdrop of a magnificent fireworks display.

At the festival I meet people from all over the country who invite me to visit them, so after it ends, I hit the road in earnest, ready to travel across the United States.

It's 1970, and California has filled a mystical place in my mind. It's portrayed as hippie heaven for the flower children of peace and love, and every hip person my age wants to be there. Everything new, exciting, and good comes from California, from deep, lovely music to pretty girls and a better way to live. I picture everyone in that magical place endlessly dancing in the sunshine with flowers in their hair.

On the West Coast, I tell myself, I will find my paradise. At last I'll experience true peace and fulfillment. My heart assures me that my quest for meaning and purpose will find answers in California.

And so I set out, reckless, happy, and confident. Thumbing rides and bumming meals and places to stay from anyone willing to help, I make my way across Oklahoma, Texas, and into New Mexico. Life on the open road feels good. I believe I'm leaving all my pain and confusion behind while California beckons with the promise of new adventures and enlightened people. The fresh air, open spaces, and big sky of the West remind me of Mexico, and I smile and dance as I stand by the roadside with my thumb out.

I love standing on the open road, looking as far into the distance as I can. From wherever I am, I imagine I see California, and it gives me hope and a reason to keep going. Something about seeing far away, into a better world, makes my present world bearable.

I write poetry, filling entire notebooks from the overflow of my heart. I pour out my pain and frustrations and write my dreams of finding answers and fulfillment in California.

I start calling Mom collect every two weeks. She knows I'm living a wild life, doing drugs and being promiscuous. Yet she always encourages me to keep searching. She ends every conversation with, "I love you."

In Oklahoma, I'm picked up by two guys headed west in a Cadillac. One evening we're invited to a party at someone's house. Outside the house we meet a guy who tells us, "The party's a biker gang. They're talking about killing you so they can steal your car." We skip the party and keep rolling west.

My practice when hitchhiking is to "work" for eight hours. I'll enter the nearest town and hitchhike back and forth through it, asking my ride if they know where I can stay the night. One evening I'm in Farmington, New Mexico. I hitchhike through town a couple of times, but no one offers me a place to stay. It's getting late when a car pulls over. An attractive young lady is driving, and a young man sits on the passenger side.

"Do you know where I could stay the night?" I ask.

"I'll take you to my family's house," the girl replies without hesitation. "We have a spare room."

I gratefully climb into the back seat, looking forward to sleeping in a real bed instead of under the stars. To my surprise, the young lady drops the young man off at his home, and we're alone in the car until we arrive at her home. Her dad is awake and offers me a soft bed in their spare bedroom for the night.

The next morning I awake and make my way into the kitchen of a simple but clean and modestly decorated home. The house is filled with aromas of toast and bacon as the mother happily prepares a hot breakfast. The father, Tom, is standing outside the kitchen door with his young son, taking turns shooting birds with a .22 caliber rifle.

The young woman who brought me the night before enters the kitchen to help her mother. She glows with simple virtue and purity. Something about this family is different.

"Are you Mormons?" I ask, picking up a *Book of Mormon* from the kitchen counter.

"Yes," Tom's wife replies with a sweet smile.

"Do your men have more than one wife?"

"No, we don't do that." She's still smiling and preparing breakfast.

After a satisfying breakfast, I'm ready to get back on the road when Tom invites me to stay a few days and help on the farm. I want to figure out why this family is so different, so I agree.

That day we load endless bales of hay onto a wagon, hauling them into the barn, then unloading and stacking them. I've never worked so hard before, and the delicious dinner fills my welcoming stomach. When I go to bed, I'm tired and aching, but happy and content.

* * * * *

One evening I tell Tom, "I admire your family. They're happy and peaceful."

"You can have that too," he responds, his gentle eyes looking into mine. "But you must first get down on your knees and find God."

"I don't want God." The God of my childhood has hurt me deeply.

On Sunday, the family brings me to their church. I've never been inside a church. The people are friendly and happy, and they all repeat Tom's message: "You need to get down on your knees and find God."

I like the people, but I wish they would stop talking about God.

On Monday morning I'm restless and ready to hit the road again. I say my farewells to my kind hosts and head out under a brilliant blue New Mexico sky. But something inside me has shifted. I believe I've found what I'm looking for—a family who really loves each other.

If only I can find a family like that who's not pushing God on me.

I continue my journey . . .

* * * * *

A couple of months later, after a few more adventures in the deserts and plains, I arrive in California. I meet plenty of hippies, but they're not who I imagined them to be. Although they proclaim peace and love, I sense dark, angry vibes from all the drugs, alcohol, sex, and pursuit of many spirits. The antiwar protests here are more violent than peaceful. Some of them are downright evil.

These people are too wild for me!

In San Francisco a guy invites me to crash at his house. In the middle of the night, he shakes me awake.

"Hey, Phil. Are you gay?"

"No," I respond, then turn over and go back to sleep.

The next morning, my host offers me orange juice and cinnamon rolls before driving me to the highway where I'll continue hitchhiking. I'm feeling something strange coming on me.

"Hey man, did you put something in those cinnamon rolls?" I ask.

"Why do you ask?"

> I haven't found people anywhere who are as happy as those poor peasants I saw in Mexico, nor as content as the dear, sweet family I stayed with in New Mexico. Practically everyone I've met these past few months is stuck in their own drama, spinning inside hamster wheels.

"I think I'm getting high."

"Just dig it, man," he advises with a smirk.

One day a guy punches me in the face after accusing me of flirting with his girlfriend. When I try to reason with him, he pulls a bayonet and swears at me, ordering me out of his sight. His punch splits my lip open, and a kind driver takes me to a hospital to get it stitched.

* * * * *

I hitchhike up the Pacific Coast to Oregon for a rock music festival. But it feels too wild and crazy—much like California. Disillusioned, I believe the West Coast is no more enlightened than anywhere else, and the people are neither more peaceful nor happy. I haven't found people anywhere who are as happy as those poor peasants I saw in Mexico, nor as content as the dear, sweet family I stayed with in New Mexico. Practically everyone I've met these past few months is stuck in their own drama, spinning inside hamster wheels that wear them out but take them nowhere.

I too am stuck in a meaningless existence. Only drugs and music offer temporary escapes from this world that's got me trapped.

* * * * *

I'm done with California and ready to get back to the calmer East Coast! I meet some students who offer me a ride east if I help them drive nonstop to Washington, D.C. For the next two and a half days we take turns driving. Exhausted, we arrive on the coast, and the students drop me off in Virginia.

After finding Jim, I hitchhike with him to Blacksburg, Virginia, where we meet some hippie college students. Most of them live off their parents' money without a care in the world. They don't mind me sponging from them, so we spend hours together. We hang out on the lawns, in the dorms, and in the town donut shop. We talk about life, get high, listen to every genre of music, play music, and read classical literature like *The Chronicles of Narnia, Catcher in the Rye,* and *One Flew Over the Cuckoo's Nest.*

This creative lifestyle fits me perfectly. I'm thinking: *Maybe I don't need a life purpose.* I'll dabble in every religion, philosophy, and drug that comes along, passively rolling with life and going nowhere. All my life I've craved acceptance. I want a place where I belong. Now I have companions. At long last I feel accepted.

I'd rather go nowhere with a crowd that's enjoying life than go somewhere with a crowd that doesn't know where they're going.

Chapter 11

REJECTION

A few days before Thanksgiving 1971, I hitchhike from Virginia to Miami to spend the holidays with my family. Predictably, it doesn't go well. Dad asks me—I mean yells at me—to leave the house. I stay in South Florida and rent a room in the same boarding house where Wally lives. I feel some security living in the same house where I believe I have at least one friend.

Two old men live there; one is missing a leg. They're down and out, society's throwaways. They spend their days sitting at an old worn-out wooden kitchen table, being together, just talking about whatever comes to mind. They're uncomplaining and gentle-spirited, and I feel peaceful and accepted. Outcasts often feel deeply for other outcasts. A fellowship of common suffering silently bonds our hearts together. I've rarely experienced compassion like I do from these two old men.

Wally helps me get a job with the same taxi company where he works, and we drive taxis all night from 5 pm to 5 am. Wally's car is number 42, and mine is 41. Even while on duty, I'm frequently high on one drug or another. One morning as I'm finishing my shift, the company's owner calls me into his office.

"Do you use heroin?" he asks bluntly.

"Naw, I just smoke a little pot," I lie.

"Well, the FBI thinks our drivers are running heroin from the air-port. They're watching you. Don't do anything stupid, and watch your step."

I'm trying to appear indifferent, but his words terrify me. I'm not running drugs like the FBI thinks, but I'm using heroin, and I know that could send me to prison.

Since I work an all-night shift, I'm supposed to sleep during the day. Back at the boarding house, I'm too nervous to sleep. A squeaky screen door slams shut and brings me bolt upright in bed, trembling with anxiety. A car door slamming on the street outside detonates pan-ic bombs inside me. I'm convinced the FBI is trailing me everywhere.

"Let's get out of here," I tell Wally. "I had a good time in Virginia, and we could go back there."

"I can't, Phil. I'm on probation for a drug charge and can't leave Florida."

Though reluctant to leave my friend, I sign up with a "drive-away" company that recruits drivers to move snowbirds' cars from Florida to their other home up north. The manager gives me twenty dollars and an Oldsmobile to deliver to a retired couple in Maryland. I push the car hard, trying to get out of Miami as quickly as possible. I keep glancing in the mirror, thinking the FBI is trailing me. After deliver-ing the car to Annapolis, Maryland without incident, I hitchhike to Virginia.

* * * * *

In Blacksburg, I find my hippie student friends. We're hanging out, playing music, getting high, and discussing life, art, philosophy, and literature. Someone helps me get a fake student ID, so I move into a campus dorm. With that ID, I'm eating in the cafeteria, using the showers, and sleeping in the dorm, all without enrolling in any class-es. Once again, I'm feeling connected and accepted. I enjoy late-night discussions on what we think life is, and jam sessions where we play music together.

I call home one day to wish Mom a happy anniversary.

"Thanks, Phil," she says, "but we're not married anymore. Your dad left with Jan, his business partner's wife. They wanted to get married, so I agreed to a divorce."

Although I'm not surprised by Dad's actions, the news further darkens my dismal memories of our family. Why does bad news follow me wherever I go?

I leave the dorm where I've been squatting and move to an old farmhouse that's for rent about 25 miles from Blacksburg. It sits in a hollow, down a long driveway out of sight of the road or any other dwellings. It's run-down, neglected, and infested with mice. The locals claim it's haunted.

A young man from New Jersey moves in with me, and we split the twenty-five-dollar rent. We purchase mousetraps and wage war on the rodents, emptying and resetting the traps every morning and evening. The constant skittering sound of mice through the house nearly drives me insane. My roommate also gets on my nerves, and I think he feels the same way about me.

The previous renters, also hippies, left their pets behind when they moved out. We inherit a big black Labrador named Pisces and a black cat named Abraxas. Their previous owners had given both animals LSD, and that left their minds messed up. Both have wild, spooky eyes. At night Abraxas prowls through the house, arching her back and meowing mournfully while rolling her eerie eyes. Pisces mostly sits staring at us from his demented eyes while giving an occasional deep growl.

One weekend, several students come to visit us in the creepy old house.

"Can you feel the evil spirits in this place?" I ask them. We sit silently, and one by one, all nod as they feel the brooding presence in the air.

"Do you want an adventure?" I ask. "Let's go up to the old grave-yard on that hill and see if we can summon the spirits."

We climb the hill and stand in a circle holding hands just outside the fence that surrounds the graveyard.

"If there are any spirits here, make yourselves known," I command.

The silence and tension build.

"We know you're there," I say.

And then a deep, moaning sound erupts behind us. Some of us collapse to the ground in terror, and I think we all stop breathing. Then we see the cows surrounding us, looking at us, like, "What are you doing here?"

Mooo . . .

Now we're laughing and trembling at the same time as we make our way down the hill and back to the house . . .

To prepare for winter, I'm spending days cutting firewood by hand with a bow saw, then splitting it with a wedge and hammer. The hard work is a contrast from my usual aimless existence, but I like doing something productive, feeling my muscles get toned and hard, and delighting in the growing firewood pile.

One day I enter the living room and discover my roommate sitting in a chair, cigarette in one hand, marijuana joint in the other. He's reading a book while the stereo blasts music, and he's built a blazing fire in the woodstove even though it's a warm day.

Something in me snaps as I watch the flames devouring the fire-wood I worked so hard to cut and split. I am thinking about killing my roommate, fantasizing exactly how I'll carry out the murder. My thoughts frighten me, and I don't know what to do with them. I see myself as a poet and dreamer, not a killer. *Where is this rage coming from?*

And then I'm hit with another bombshell.

* * * * *

Some folks in a small commune a few miles away invite me to join them for Thanksgiving. I borrow their phone and call Mom collect. After a couple of "How are you?" exchanges, Mom says, "Your friend Wally is dead."

"What!" I exclaim. "No, there must be a mistake!"

"I'll read you the newspaper article. I knew he was your friend, so I cut it out for you."

She reads Wally's full name, and I know Mom's right. He had been robbed while driving his taxi. Someone shot my gentle friend in the head several times for the few dollars in his pocket. Apparently, that's how much Wally's life was worth: five or ten dollars.

Why does everyone I care about die? First Uncle Bert, then my childhood friend, Scotty, was playing Dare Me with a partially loaded gun in a circle of friends and blew his brains out. Now Wally. And where are they now? Is death the end, or are they alive somewhere? For days and weeks I mourn the loss of my tall, skinny, thoughtful musician friend. Through my tears I smile as I remember how Wally liked to wear clothes with vertical stripes that made him look even taller.

"I'm a mile long!" he'd say with a grin.

* * * * *

Still grieving Wally's death, I hitchhike to Atlanta to see Dad and his new wife, Janice.

"My friend Wally was murdered," I tell Dad, inviting him into my grief.

"These things happen," Dad says with a shrug. If he feels any sympathy for me, he doesn't know how to express it.

As I watch Dad and Janice bitterly fighting—just as he and Mom used to—I feel both disgusted and vindicated. For my dad, only his victim has changed; everything else about his endless, bickering life remains.

"You can stay in our spare room," Dad offers. "I own a gas station, and you can work for me."

For years Dad had been telling me, "You're not a real man until you can beat me in a fight." One day, while working at his gas station, Dad accuses me of something I didn't do and refuses to accept my explanation.

"Either fight me or get out!" he screams into my face; he's so close I can smell the mingled odors of whiskey, tobacco, and sweat.

I gather my few belongings and walk out. As I stand in the dimly lit parking lot outside the apartment complex where Dad lives, I shudder all over and ask myself, *When will I stop running away?*

Summoning all my nerve, I return to the apartment and, with a trembling hand, knock on the door. When Dad opens it, I raise my shaking fists and say, "I'm ready to fight!"

Dad stares at me for a long moment. Then he releases a deep sigh, his shoulders slump, and his head droops in defeat as the blood drains from his face. I've called his bluff, and the angry, domineering brute I've always known melts in front of me into a broken, feeble wretch. My challenge has exposed him, and shame sweeps over both of us as though I have revealed his nakedness. Dad drops heavily into a kitchen chair and buries his face in his trembling hands. The last traces of control have been stripped from him. I take no pleasure in his humiliation.

"Please take me to Grady Hospital," he begs hoarsely.

Once he checks in and is evaluated, the hospital staff tell me Dad is having a mental breakdown. They ask me to sign the forms to admit him into the psychiatric ward. I pick up the pen, but I can't bring myself to sign.

I look up and see Dad at the end of the hospital corridor, limping toward me. Years of drug and alcohol abuse have damaged him physically and mentally. His hair, which always was impeccably styled, is now disheveled and dirty, as are his clothes. Dad's eyes stare wildly at me, his face a muted cry for help.

I don't remember the drive back to the house, but we get there somehow.

I try to sleep, but toss and turn until morning. When Dad gets up, it's like nothing happened. If I think calling his bluff means we're now equals, I'm mistaken.

* * * * *

A few days later I'm goofing around with another gas station employee. That night, after work, Dad furiously accuses me of making fun of him.

"I saw you guys mocking me out by the pumps today."

"Dad, we were goofing off. We weren't even talking about you."

"You were mocking me!" he insists, his face distorted with rage.

"Honestly, we weren't."

"Get out!" he demands.

Weary of arguing, I leave. My clothes are insufficient for the freezing temperatures that night, but that's not why I'm shaking uncontrollably. I feel the old familiar rejection. Once more, I'm discarded like a piece of garbage.

Wearily, I thumb rides from Atlanta back to Virginia.

My crazy roommate has moved out while I was gone, so now I'm alone in the old house with the mice, the psychotic dog and cat, and worst of all, my own thoughts. I can't stop the endless brain chatter from spiraling me ever deeper into despair as rejection gnaws at my soul.

Chapter 12

PRIMAL SCREAMS AND PEACE UNDER THE WATERFALL

Then I meet Steve. He is as calm and easygoing as I am volatile. Steve wants to move in with me. I wonder: *Why would anyone want to live with me?* I don't ask him. Instead, I welcome him into the weird old haunted house.

Steve and I often talk into the wee hours. I tell him my darkest thoughts and fears, and to my surprise, he doesn't reject me or call me crazy.

After a few months we move to a lovely old farm a few miles away that's perfect for a hippie lifestyle. This two-story farmhouse is old and run down, situated in a beautiful spot on 200 acres of thistle-infested pastureland. A faded picket fence surrounds the front yard, which is shaded by a huge mulberry tree. The house is secluded at the end of a long lane and out of sight of any neighbors. It doesn't have indoor plumbing, so we carry water up the hill from a cool, sweet spring.

When Steve and I move into the place, we bring the crazy black lab, Pisces, and another dog named Animal that someone gave us. Pisces and Animal fight all the time.

The day before we move in, Mr. Barker, the farmer who owns the place, purchased fifty young feeder pigs to graze and eat grain from feeders he placed around the farm. When the pigs grow large enough, they'll be sold at market.

The morning after Steve and I move to the farm, we wake to the snarling sounds of Pisces and Animal fighting. We step outside and see the two dogs in a ferocious tug-of-war with a little feeder pig between them as the prize. When we run out to separate them, we see dead little pigs everywhere.

A few hours later, Mr. Barker shows up, and man, is he upset! He shakes his head and says we'll have to pay twenty dollars each for the ten dead pigs. Steve and I decide to butcher the meat to recover some of our cost. We go to a neighbor, who loans us a couple of knives and explains how to gut, skin, and cut the little piggies into meat.

The neighbor says to salt the meat and hang it up to cure if we want it to keep. So Steve and I hang the hams from ropes on the back porch. We shake some salt from a shaker over the hanging meat, not realizing we're supposed to soak the meat in a thick salt brine. After a few weeks, the spoiling meat stinks to high heaven.

Steve and I become vegetarians.

Soon two acquaintances, Jim and Rachel, join us at the farm. Now we officially call ourselves a hippie commune. Rachel names it Planet Earth and paints the name on a pretty little sign we plant next to the mailbox.

I spend most of my time writing poetry and playing guitar. Soaking in the serenity of our rural setting, I create soft, soothing melodies. Jim borrows my guitar and bellows out songs, pounding the instrument so hard he breaks strings and gashes the guitar with pick marks. Whenever Jim confronts one of us about anything, he gets a wild look in his eyes, shoves his nose against ours, and gives us a stern lecture.

While Jim is volatile, Rachel is simply insane. I don't mean figuratively; her insanity is well documented. She's been in and out of mental institutions. I think she takes pleasure in her mental instability and wears the label like a badge of honor.

Many people drift in and out of Planet Earth. Steve always remains calm, an unruffled fortress amid the chaos. He helps us maintain a peaceful atmosphere, and I settle into a routine of writing poetry, playing guitar, and entertaining visitors. We also visit our neighbors and wander around the 200-acre farm.

When spring comes, we want to plant a garden. Unfortunately, none of us knows how to garden, so Steve and I visit a neighbor for advice. He loans us a hoe and shows us how to use it.

Then, in all sincerity, I ask, "How do you plant a garden?"

He gets a mischievous twinkle in his eye and is probably thinking, *Dumb city kid!*

With one tobacco-swollen cheek and a smirk on his face, he half mumbles, "You put the seed in the ground."

I blush, and everything goes silent between us.

* * * * *

By now I've had several girlfriends, but I'm longing for someone to spend my life with. One day I have a premonition that I'm going to meet my future wife in about a month. The drugs I'm taking do many strange tricks with my mind, but this impression hits me much stronger than my drug-induced fantasies. I think about it frequently.

One morning about a month later, I wake up feeling that today is the day. A friend, Craig, comes to visit me. We stroll through the farm's rolling hills, chatting as we walk.

"I'm going to meet my wife today," I tell Craig, who quietly smiles. After our walk, he gives me a ride into Blacksburg. There I meet an attractive young brunette named Nancy.

"Hey, I'm supposed to meet my wife today," I tell her. "Is that you?"

"No, I already have a boyfriend," she replies with a laugh. "But he doesn't mind if we hang out."

We spend a pleasant day together, and I repeat my question to Nancy several times, but she insists she's not my wife. After a dance at the university student center that evening, we stroll back onto the deserted streets as midnight approaches.

I'm puzzled; the premonition about meeting my wife on this day has felt so strong, but the day is nearly over. Once more, I ask Nancy, "Are you sure you're not my wife?"

Nancy laughs and shakes her head. "Don't worry," she says. "Maybe you'll meet her tomorrow."

And then, like in a scene from a movie, we see a lone figure walking toward us. She slowly shuffles along the sidewalk with greasy red hair, beady brown eyes behind granny glasses, brown corduroy pants, and a white T-shirt. Her shoulders are slumped, and she's clearly exhausted.

"Hey, there's Gina!" Nancy exclaims, gesturing toward the lone figure.

"Hi, Nancy," Gina (pronounced Jenna) says as we stroll toward each other.

There she is, the silent voice in my head whispers. But I also think: *Well, that's not exactly what I was expecting.* I look more closely at Gina, trying to figure out if she's the one or not.

"Gina, this is Phil," Nancy says. "We've been out walking. Why are you out so late by yourself?"

"I just finished work at the sub shop, and I don't have a way home," Gina responds.

"Do you live nearby?" I ask her.

Gina shakes her head. "No, I live with my brother on a farm forty-five minutes out of town."

Nancy invites both of us to her place. "Come home with us. Phil is going to crash on the couch, and we have room for you too."

We walk the few blocks to Nancy's house where she introduces her boyfriend, Bryce, who's strumming a guitar. He welcomes us both, predictably unruffled when Nancy announces that Gina and I are spending the night. I pick up another guitar and accompany him while watching Gina from the corner of my eye. I'm now starting to believe she's going to be my wife, and I want to get to know her.

When Gina leaves the room for a bit, Nancy explains that Gina has recently come from teaching Chicano and Indian children near a reservation in New Mexico.

"Plus, she recently broke up with her boyfriend," Nancy says. "She needs someone to care for her."

That sounds good to me. I'll be her rescuer, her Prince Charming. She returns to the room and I'm fantasizing about romancing Gina with my guitar.

"You want to watch us play?" I ask, fully expecting a smiling yes.

Gina shakes her head. "I'm too tired. I just want to sleep."

She heads to bed despite Nancy's urgings to hang out with us.

Not a very promising start, I think. I shrug my shoulders and return to playing guitar.

The next morning welcomes a beautiful Virginia summer day, so Bryce, Nancy, Gina, and I drive to the mountains to enjoy the perfect weather. Gina appears much more relaxed and at ease than she was last night.

I plunge into a mountain stream at the base of a waterfall, then extend a hand to Gina and call, "Come on in!"

She wades in to join me, and I take her hand and lead her under the cascading falls. We laugh in delight and splash each other like carefree children. I feel drawn to her, and I believe that, at long last, my heart has found a home.

Gina is quiet and reserved, and her presence brings me deep serenity. As we linger through this magical day together—it's the summer of 1973—I'm eager to learn more about her.

"I grew up in Baton Rouge, Louisiana," she tells me. "I graduated from Southern Methodist University with a double degree in math and education. Last year I taught math to junior high students in Taos, New Mexico."

"Wow, that's an impressive list of accomplishments!"

Gina shakes her head modestly. "It didn't bring any meaning or purpose to my life. The closest I've come to happiness is living with my brother Hank on his rented farm. He's raising chickens, pigs, and goats, and I help him with gardening. I also have a potter's wheel, and I'm learning pottery. That gives me more peace than anything else."

We're sitting side by side on a big rock, listening to the roar and watching the hypnotic flow of the crystal-clear, sparkling curtain of water in front of us.

"So have you found peace?" I ask. "Have you figured out what your purpose is?"

Gina smiles and gives a little shrug. "Can anyone ever say they've filled the emptiness inside? Is that possible?"

I shrug. "Sometimes I get weary of the search. But I keep looking. Right now, I'm trying to find fulfillment in little things, like living in the country."

* * * * *

Gina moves into Planet Earth with me while continuing her part-time job at the sub shop. We want a car for travel and adventure together, so we pay two hundred dollars for an old Ford Fairlane. The car has been wrecked, and the right front fender is primed but unpainted, so Gina and I purchase a gallon of lime green house paint and brush-paint the entire car green.

We're driving in city traffic one day when . . . *BAM!* A middle-aged woman driving a midget convertible sports car slams into our rear end. She gets out holding a little Chihuahua, scared the little guy might be hurt. A couple of days later the insurance adjuster comes out, looks at the car, and declares it totaled. He hands me a check for two hundred and fifty dollars, or fifty more than we paid for it, but we continue driving the car. The damaged rear end leaves the trunk latch broken, so I keep it closed with a bungee cord. Often the cord comes loose, and the trunk lid flops up and down as we drive.

I purchase cheap, used, mismatched tires for the car, and this causes it to wobble down the road like a lopsided crab. Inside, the black ceiling upholstery is falling down, so we fasten it up with thumbtacks. But when we drive with the windows open, the draft rips the thumbtacks out, causing the upholstery to billow and flap against our heads. We're probably quite a sight, wobbling down the road with the trunk lid bouncing and headliner flapping. But we don't care, we're happy together.

Or so we think.

Gina and I quickly learn that we have little in common except our search for something better than our empty, superficial lives. In every other way our lives are, and have been, different. Gina was raised in a stable home in a peaceful southern Louisiana neighborhood, surrounded by kindhearted people who cared for each other. I grew up in a violently dysfunctional home in rough inner-city neighborhoods.

Her parents and siblings are all high achievers who graduated with honors from top universities and have, or are pursuing, illustrious careers. Gina graduated from SMU with a double degree, near the top of her college class. My relatives are mostly underachievers, and I graduated near the bottom of my high school class of about eight hundred. I went to college but never finished.

Gina's home was calm and peaceful; she has no memories of anyone getting angry. By contrast, I never knew life without constant outbursts of rage and violence. Even with Gina's calming influence in my life, I'm volatile and angry.

Full of rage, I deliberately pursue pain. Pain is familiar, and in it I find my only security. So I pursue painful music, painful drugs, painful memories, and painful relationships. I abuse myself—body, mind, emotions—until I'm twisted into a grotesque, raging monster.

> I pursue painful music, painful drugs, painful memories, and painful relationships. I abuse myself—body, mind, emotions— until I'm twisted into a grotesque, raging monster.

My mind chatters relentlessly, sometimes erupting into raging migraine headaches that incapacitate me for days, making me so sick I need to retreat into a dark room and sometimes throw up. The slightest noise or motion triggers explosions in my head.

I try numbing my restless, hurting brain with drugs: psychedelics, barbiturates, speed, marijuana, alcohol, and tobacco. Wild music and sex fail to soothe my soul, so I explore Eastern religions and the occult. I steal things for the quick rush it gives me.

I'm trying to imitate poets and musicians whose pain and rage earned them recognition, from Edgar Allen Poe to John Lennon, Jimi Hendrix, and Janis Joplin. I've declared myself the king of pain; I try to out-pain everyone I meet. Unable to make people love me, I manipulate them into relationships by using my pain to draw sympathy from them. Inevitably, I burn out their friendship, accumulating new layers of pain inside myself, bringing even more pain into each new relationship, and then repeating the cycle.

Sometimes the dark voices in my head try to torment me into doing unspeakable, evil acts. I visit a psychiatrist, who administers a battery of personality tests.

"You're filled with hostility," she concludes. "You need to check yourself into a mental hospital before you seriously hurt someone."

I stare at the psychiatrist, an overweight little woman wearing thick makeup and puffing a cigarette as we talk.

How can she help me with my problems? I wonder. *She hides behind a layer of makeup and a cigarette smokescreen. If I get help, I want it from someone who's real.*

Primal screaming is popular among hippies, so we try it at Planet Earth. The violent scream is supposed to release a lifetime of suppressed pain and restore our childhood innocence. It feels good, so we don't limit our screams to just when we're at Planet Earth. Without forethought or warning, we throw our heads back and howl like wolves with thorns in their paws—no matter where we are.

The primal screams feel especially good when we're in public. We watch the funny reactions of strangers while we're driving down the road. At the first shriek, people jump and spin around, their wide eyes desperately trying to locate the source of the hideous noise. When they spot the hippie with his nose pointing to the sky and his mouth opened in a quavering howl, their fear usually gives way to amusement or disgust.

Even though primal screams feel good in the moment, the darkness soon surges back in. Searching for a lasting solution, we try days of fasting and silence. For days, we don't eat or talk. When we want to communicate, we scribble brief messages on a notepad. However, our monastic silence and appetite denial provides only temporary relief and the illusion of true peace.

I've built a platform bed for myself about three feet off the floor. I hang a curtain around the bed to create an enclosed space underneath. Sometimes I withdraw into my little cave and ponder my hopeless, empty, lonely life. My body convulses with sobs until my tears are dry and I can no longer cry, but my soul continues weeping.

I wander through the woods and scream until I'm hoarse. I scream at God: "Where are you!? Why don't you give me answers!? Do you exist!?" The God of my childhood is somewhere far away and silent. Screaming releases pressure, but nothing in my life changes.

Worst of all, I scream at Gina. Although I love her and know meeting her is the best thing that ever happened to me, I can't stop myself.

Gina never experienced anger in her peaceful home, and my violent outbursts terrify her. Emotionally paralyzed by my rage, she withdraws like a turtle into a hard shell and looks for opportunities to get away from me.

When I'm not consumed with rage, Gina and I enjoy wonderful times together. The bonds we forge during those good times somehow hold us together through the hard times. Still looking for answers to life's basic questions, we experiment with Hinduism, transcendental meditation, and the do-it-yourself hippie religions of the 1970s—but nothing is helping.

We're still two lost souls. But at least now we're wandering together.

Chapter 13

LITTLE COUNTRY CHURCH

Gina and I continue wandering around the country in our battered green Ford. We spend a few months in Richmond, Virginia in the basement of an old apartment building. The space has been converted into a makeshift apartment, with many exposed pipes on the walls and ceilings from the building's plumbing system. With our friend Steve, we're interested in becoming house painters, so we practice by painting the pipes a wild variety of pastel colors.

In one of the apartments above us, we befriend a married couple in their thirties. I sometimes hang out with them, talking endlessly about my explorations into Eastern religions and philosophies, transcendental meditation, and vegetarianism. I'm constantly pushing my beliefs, and the husband displays amazing patience as he listens to my idealistic ramblings. But one night, even his store of patience becomes exhausted.

Taking advantage of a momentary pause in my lecturing, he firmly says, "Go live your beliefs for ten years. Then come back, and if they're working for you, I'll be ready to listen."

His words hit me hard, yet I know he's right. When we leave Richmond to continue our nomadic lifestyle, I'm determined to take his challenge: I want to find a way of believing and living that works for at least ten years.

* * * * *

We drift from place to place, eventually landing in a commune in Atlanta that owns a macrobiotic health food restaurant. While there, a friend asks us for a ride to a commune called Lighthouse Ridge in Tennessee. The commune is down an old stagecoach trail, seven miles from the nearest road, and it's pouring rain the night we arrive. We get deep stuck in the mud and have to ditch the van and be rescued and shuttled into the commune by a four-wheel-drive Land Rover. As the rain continues, we're stranded at Lighthouse Ridge for several more days.

We quickly get to know the people in the commune. The Ridge covers about 70 acres along the edge of the Cumberland Plateau mountain range, and it's home to about a dozen people who come and go. Several of them live in an old school bus with a log lean-to attached. One young man lives alone on the side of the mountain under a homemade tent made from tree branches and clear plastic, while an older man stays in a travel trailer. A disillusioned Vietnam veteran lives a hermit lifestyle deep in the woods outside the commune in a crude shelter he built from saplings, plastic wrap, and salvaged tin.

The Ridge is owned by a man I'll call Carlos, a tall, lean Latin American. Although a keen and dynamic leader, he's too restless to stay put and often is gone from the commune he's supposed to lead. In his absence, chaos reigns among our tribe of dropouts and misfits. Despite the chaos, Gina and I think we've discovered hippie heaven and settle in to stay.

We've dreamed of living off the land in harmony with nature, and now we've found it in the backwoods of Tennessee. The Ridge has no electricity, plumbing, or telephones, but we don't mind. We're basking

The Ridge has no electricity, plumbing, or telephones, but we don't mind. We're basking in an oasis of music, drugs, and free love, seven miles from a materialistic world.

in an oasis of music, drugs, and free love, seven miles from a materialistic world. Still, we need to purchase food, and our group survives only because folks receive money from inheritances, alimony checks, welfare, food stamps, or selling drugs. Occasionally someone attends a craft show and sells the hippie jewelry and leather crafts we make in our little shop on the property.

The locals tolerate us as long as we keep to ourselves, although they see us as long-haired freaks who can't be trusted. The sheriff's department keeps a wary eye on us, sometimes pulling over our vehicles when we're in town or coming out to the commune to search our dwellings.

One day while driving in town, a deputy stops and arrests me because my old green Ford has expired Virginia plates. Such trivial offenses usually don't warrant arrest, but the police want us to know we're not welcome here.

The deputy takes me to the county jail where the sheriff personally escorts me to a cell. As we walk down the corridor, he shocks me by looking into my eyes and saying, "I have faith in you. I think you can make it."

I can't believe my ears. Apart from Uncle Bert, I can't recall anyone who has ever believed in me. Dad pounded into my head that I'm a worthless monster who will die in a gutter. For one precious moment, a ray of hope, a shaft of light, touches my soul. A rundown old jail is a most unlikely place to find a glimmer of hope, and yet, as I'm marching to my cell, the sheriff's faith makes me believe—for a moment, at least—that maybe I'm more than a failure.

"Thanks, Sheriff," I say, welling up with tears.

The jail is more than one hundred years old, and my cell resembles a medieval dungeon. The tarnished bars and concrete furnishings are quaint in a way, but I hear echoes of the ghosts of past prisoners, and I know depression will soon overtake me in this place.

So this is how it feels to be a criminal, I muse. *I've become a lot of ugly things, and now I'm a criminal.* When I reflect on all my stealing and illegal drug use, I must admit I deserve that label. I've broken the law many times, always without getting caught.

After a few hours in the cell, a local attorney who sympathizes with our commune bails me out. I purchase Tennessee plates for the car and pay a fine at my subsequent court appearance.

* * * * *

When the locals discover that we welcome African-Americans into our commune, their tolerance abruptly ends. Racism is deeply entrenched in the local Bible Belt culture, and when news spreads about a couple of young black people visiting us, neighbors threaten to burn down our buildings and drive us out.

We hold an emergency meeting to discuss our options. Since Gina and I are into everything spiritual—from transcendental meditation to Buddhism to drugs, music, horoscopes, and tarot—the commune members think we're the obvious choice to establish a relationship with local churches. So the group delegates Gina and me to make peace with our neighbors by attending their churches.

Gina and I agree. We'll begin with the local Mennonites. We've encountered these reclusive, old-fashioned people several times and know they live simply, dress in outdated clothing, farm with simple machinery, and have large families. Two men from their church had come to the commune and tried to preach to us, but we were super hostile toward them, mocking and cursing the Jesus they tried to share with us. Despite our hostility, the Mennonites are good neighbors who often lend us tools or bring their tractors to pull our vehicles out of the mud.

The Sunday after our emergency meeting, Gina and I ride horses more than seven miles from the commune to the unadorned cement block building that's a rural Mennonite church house. The gravel parking lot is filled with black vehicles, which, combined with the spartan building, create a somber mood.

The service is already underway, so we try slipping in unobtrusively through the side door. As I open the door, the old hinges squeak loudly, and all eyes in the building fix on us as we enter. The men and women are sitting on opposite sides of the room, and we enter from the men's side. A freckle-faced man with a red beard slides sideways on the bench to make room for me, and Gina shuffles past the men to find a seat on the women's side.

I gaze around, fascinated by this alien world. The women's side is filled with rows of long, dark dresses and white caps. On the men's side, row after row of men and boys wearing identical black suspenders form a symmetrical art pattern in my mind. As I look around at the somber men with their dark shirts buttoned all the way to the top and their long sleeves, I realize how strange I must appear to them with my ponytail, shorts, T-shirt, and sandals. The contrast between Gina in her bib overalls and flip-flops and the women in their ankle-length dresses and white caps is even more startling.

The man behind the pulpit speaks about living by the Golden Rule, that Christians never should harm other people. When he reads verses from his Bible, something inside me lights up.

Nothing in this building is remotely decorative or ornate. Most of the finish is worn away from the plain hardwood floors, and the cement block walls are unpainted. The windows have old-fashioned roller blinds, drawn partway down each window.

A dark-haired bearded man stands behind the simple, varnished, particle board pulpit, preaching to about fifty adults and many more children and teens. My strange surroundings captivate me, but the sermon captures me even more.

The man behind the pulpit speaks about living by the Golden Rule, that Christians never should harm other people. When he reads verses from his Bible, something inside me lights up.

After several minutes, a rustling sound suddenly spreads through the building. People turn to kneel with their elbows propped on the wooden benches where they were sitting a moment before. I hurry to imitate them, and we kneel through a long prayer. When it ends, everyone resumes their seats, and someone calls out a song number. As people open the songbooks, a man begins to sing, and soon the congregation joins in. The slow, gentle melodies remind me of synagogue singing, and yet it's not the same.

When the service ends, the red-haired man next to me introduces himself with a friendly smile. Then he asks, "Are you a Christian?"

"Yeah," I quickly lie, hoping to stop him from probing any deeper.

Another slightly older bearded man approaches with a broad, welcoming smile and a few gold-capped teeth glistening, "Would you join us for lunch?" he asks as he shakes my hand with a firm, farmer's grip. I notice he's missing a finger.

Wow, this is going to be a real adventure, I think. "Sure," I answer, "we'll come if Gina wants to."

We leave the horses tied at the church house and someone from the family gives us a ride to their home a few miles away.

The father and sons gather in the living room chatting with Gina and me. The older daughters help their mother prepare the meal. Apparently, the kitchen is the women's domain.

Soon we're joining them around the long table in their spacious dining room.

"Are these all your children?" I ask, looking around the crowded table.

"Yes, we have eleven," our host's wife replies.

My eyes widen in disbelief. *Eleven* children? How is that possible? After the father says a prayer, the wife hands a platter of sliced bread to her husband. He silently removes a slice, places it on his plate, and passes the bread to the child next to him. The little boy takes a slice with the same silent concentration, as does each child in turn. I think this could be a sacred ritual, so I imitate their motions as I take a slice and pass the plate.

When they pass the mashed potatoes and green beans, Gina asks, "Do you have a garden? Do you raise all these vegetables?"

"Oh yes," the wife laughs. "We raise everything we eat. I don't know what we'd do without our garden."

Next comes a huge platter of meatloaf. Although Gina and I are now vegetarians because we think it's kinder to our fellow creatures, the aroma of that meatloaf tempts us beyond endurance. As it passes from hand to hand around the table, Gina and I look at each other silently: *what should we do?*

The boy next to me places a large meatloaf square on his plate. Steam rises from it, seductive and fragrant. Impulsively, I take a piece and pass the platter. When the meat reaches Gina, I'm relieved to see her also take a serving.

Then I take my first bite. *M-m-m-m.* I don't care how strange these people are; this meatloaf more than makes up for it. Every bite is sheer pleasure, and I see Gina's enjoyment matching mine.

After we finish eating, the father says, "Let's return thanks." They close their eyes and bow their heads in silent prayer.

* * * * *

On our way back to the commune, Gina and I compare impressions of our remarkable day.

"That meatloaf was incredible!" I nearly shout.

"I thought so, too," she says with a laugh.

"Let's go back sometime," I said. "They seem like nice people, and maybe we'll get some more of that good cooking."

We can't explain it, but we both feel a warm glow inside after our time with these simple yet remarkable people. Obviously, these kind-hearted folks aren't the ones threatening to burn down our buildings and run us off the mountain!

Although they no longer seem a threat, our curiosity draws Gina and me back to church a few weeks later. The second visit still feels foreign, but we somewhat know what to expect and don't feel as out of place.

Again, we receive an invitation to join a family for lunch, this time for a meal of chicken they raised and butchered themselves.

Gina and I silently apologize to the chickens who gave their lives to satisfy us greedy humans—but that doesn't stop us from enjoying the delicious meat.

Chapter 14

THE PRODIGAL

As Gina and I befriend the Mennonites, our initial apprehensions dissolve, and we feel kinship with them. After all, we have some things in common. They—and we—reject mainstream society. They—and we—choose to stand out with unusual clothing.

We have our differences too. Their church has strict rules that regulate every detail of their lives, while we're lawless, freethinking, unstructured hippies. Still, we're all outsiders and misfits to the world, which we think will create a bond between us.

One Saturday afternoon the church arranges an outdoor service especially for us hippies. We meet at Mill Cove, a breathtakingly beautiful spot on a bluff overlooking a wooded valley.

The church people bring chairs to the outdoor service while we hippies sit cross-legged, yoga style, on the ground. As they sing, the nearby waterfall provides a musical backdrop as water cascades over the rocks 100 feet to the valley below. Nature's splendor combined with the beauty and grace of our hosts' a cappella singing gently opens my heart.

As the deacon describes a story from the book of Luke, of the prodigal son, I sit spellbound. The Bible is unlike anything I've ever read in classical literature, mystical books, or even Hebrew school.

He tells of a young man who runs away from home and wastes his inheritance on "riotous living." The young man descends into despair, then comes to his senses and goes home to his father. The father welcomes the prodigal with love, acceptance, and open arms.

His beautiful story captivates me, but as I look at my life, my heart breaks. Whenever I try going home to my father, I meet the same rage and rejection. The deacon tells the story of a father who loves his son, and tears trickle down my cheeks at this glimpse of what I've never had.

Even as my tears flow, something stirs deep inside me. I try fighting off my deeper emotions. I can't let myself get sucked into this. Although these people are Christians—and that must mean they're Jew-haters—I'm overwhelmed with longing for a father who would welcome me home with open arms. But surely, there must be a way to do that without Jesus!

Although I've rejected my Jewish upbringing, I can't forget what the rabbis drilled into me: "The Jesus of the Christians is not our Messiah. The *goyim* [Gentiles] need a Messiah because they're separated from God. We have never been separated from God."

Despite the wide chasm I feel between them and me, I'm strangely drawn to these gentle people. It makes no sense; why would a wild, psychedelic, freewheeling hippie like me be drawn to such disciplined, pious people? It's partly their simple lifestyle. But even more, it's their families. Ever since I encountered the Mormon family in New Mexico, I've dreamed of a stable, loving family. I experienced a taste of Heaven in their home, and now I think I've found it again.

My mind drifts back to the commune in Atlanta where Gina and I lived before we wandered into Lighthouse Ridge. We all were enthusiastic about Eastern mystic religions, chanting Om, doing yoga, and eating a strict macrobiotic diet, and we had a lot in common with the

Hare Krishna sect. Yet behind the masks of our spirituality, we had serious clashes.

We couldn't even agree on how to start our meetings.

"We all should chant 'Om,'" someone suggested.

"No, let's pray," someone else said.

"Who would we pray to?"

"How about we observe a moment of silence?"

"Hey, let's start the meeting!"

After about an hour of bickering, the meeting broke up before it started.

These church people aren't like that. They all appear to get along, believing, dressing, and living the same way. I can't imagine them arguing over how to begin a meeting—or, for that matter, anything else.

While I ponder these strange people, the service ends. The women set out the home-cooked meal they have brought to share with us. I'm touched by their willingness to conduct an outdoor service for us hippies. And, of course, Gina and I enjoy the delicious food they bring.

These gentle people are reaching out to us, offering us the truths they believe we lack. I can't shake my strange attraction to them and their simple lifestyle. Gina and I continue attending their church, and one Sunday the sermon is titled "Love at Home."

The pastor describes a home where people love each other—not as a wishful fantasy, but as though he's describing a familiar daily life that he's actually experiencing. His message tugs deep and hard at my heart, and I have no words. Images of my childhood flood my mind. I see Mom and Dad fighting, screaming insults, cursing each other. I wince at the memories of Dad's beatings and his angry shouts telling me I'm a monster who'll die in a gutter.

Tears spill from my eyes as the pastor talks simply and matter-of-factly about God wanting every home to become a taste of Heaven on earth. My mind flashes back to Dad forcing me to strip naked in front of my mom and siblings, and then lashing me with his belt. Then he spits in my face and walks away. The memories still sting me, and fresh tears course down my cheeks.

I long for a home like the preacher is describing, a family of loving people who care for each other. But I can't shake those childhood flashbacks, and I shake my head in despair.

It's no use, I think. *I'll never have a home like that. These people can do it because they're naturally good, but I'm too evil.*

After the message ends, they sing a hymn with the same title as the sermon: "Love at Home."

> *There is beauty all around*
> *When there's love at home.*
> *There is joy in every sound.*
> *When there's love at home.*

I want to experience love at home! I think. *But I wish they would quit talking about God. Why would God help me? I've done too much wrong.*

Before the closing prayer, the preacher extends an invitation: "If you want to experience love like this, please rise to your feet."

Feeling alone, dirty, and rejected, I sit on the old wooden bench, shaking with sobs because I know I'm too damaged for even God to fix!

* * * * *

Soon afterward, Gina wants to spend Christmas with her family in New Jersey. Peter, one of our new church friends, offers to drive her to the airport. I ride along with Peter and his wife. On the way home we stop at a mall to do some shopping, and I notice a store that sells rare coins.

"My buddy Mike and I used to steal coins from a store like that," I tell Peter. "One of us distracted the clerk while the other shoplifted from the other side of the store. We got some valuable coins that way."

I laugh at the memory, but Peter doesn't. He looks at me thoughtfully and says, "Someday, when you know the truth, you'll go back and pay for everything you stole."

His gentle words cut deep into my heart. He doesn't say I'll make restitution if I ever know the truth. He's confident someday I *will* know the truth.

On the drive home, I'm thinking about all the stuff I have stolen or borrowed (and never returned) and all the people I've wronged. There's no way I'll ever be able to pay back everything!

There's no way God will ever let me become a Christian! And yet, I can't shake the suffocating guilt. The accumulation of a lifetime of wrongdoing crushes me under its weight.

"You're really quiet," Peter observes. "What's wrong?"

I'm too tormented to answer, but I know what's wrong. I'm facing the reality of who I am. I've always craved authenticity and reality in people, but now I hate my reality—a broken, dirty, sinful young man who's destroying myself and everyone else.

* * * * *

Over the next few days, I can't shake my heavy guilt. Everyone else from Lighthouse Ridge has left to spend Christmas with family or friends, so I'm alone. I take long walks in the woods, wrestling with questions that torment me.

One day I'm walking alone in the woods when a strange sensation comes over me. I feel God's presence and his love and perfection. He's pure, and I'm filthy. Despite this, I feel his love for me. He loves *me*? I can't understand how a perfect God would love someone as bad as me, but I'm feeling it too deeply to doubt him.

He's inviting me to accept his love! How foolish to continue my sinful, self-destructive life when God's offering more than I could ever dream!

But what about Jesus? Jews are supposed to hate him, and what will my family think if I accept Jesus? I'm torn between my Jewish heritage and my longing to accept God's love for me.

Suddenly, I don't care what anyone thinks. I need a Father's love, and that's what God is offering me. If Jesus is the way to God, I'm willing to accept him.

I kneel on the cool, damp ground of the Tennessee woods.

"Father, I've been running away from Dad, but I'm becoming like him and destroying myself because I'm actually running away from You. Please forgive me for running from Dad and from You. Please come into my life and forgive my sins. If accepting Jesus is the only way You'll accept me, I'll do it."

Something happens inside me as I pray those words. An incredible peace washes over me. Sweet tears fill my eyes. I lift my face toward the sky, and the gentle sun warms my face and dries my tears. A soft breeze whispers through the trees, and I stare around in amazement.

It's so simple. In less than a minute and a half, I know something inside me has changed.

I walk back to the commune with light steps, breathing the fresh air of freedom and weeping tears of joy. I feel like a new person! Does following Jesus make me a Mennonite . . . or am I still a Jew . . . or still a hippie?

I don't know, but my heart's glowing.

Chapter 15

RESTITUTION AND RECONCILIATION

The hippies in our commune see the change in me—and to my surprise, they respond with contempt. Despite all the hippie rhetoric about love, peace, and acceptance, they refuse to tolerate the new Phil.

Now I don't need to escape into drugs. Instead, I'm working with my hands, cutting firewood, cleaning up, and fixing stuff around the crude barn where I live. I finish each day feeling satisfied. Although I've become a more productive member of the commune, they're rejecting me. They sneer at me for becoming one of "those weird religious people." Some of them steal my firewood, and I'm getting the message that I'm not welcome. I need to move on.

The following Sunday I come to the Mennonite church glowing and expecting a great celebration at my conversion. When I tell them what happened, some cordially smile, while others respond with suspicion. Their doubt hurts me, but I know God has changed me, and I'm now determined to live for him.

Soon the Miller family offers me a home. I gratefully move into a house already overflowing with eight children—seven boys and a girl. (They originally had thirteen children: four have married and one died.)

They give me my own room, three meals a day, and the opportunity to experience love at home. I observe them closely, eager to learn all I can about Christian family living.

My hosts are dairy farmers who also raise their own crops. They work together, enjoying their labors and each other. I tag along with the father and sons, trying to make myself useful, and I'm amazed at how well the boys get along. The rolling Tennessee hills remind me of the Mexican countryside, and I believe I've found people like those simple, serene Mexican peasants who had touched me so deeply.

Although my presence is creating more work for her, Mrs. Miller joyfully accepts me. She makes me feel like I belong and promises to pray for me as she does for her own children.

From the start the family includes me in their worship times when we read a Bible chapter, sing, and pray together after breakfast. The older boys spend many evenings singing together in their bedroom. They're not trained musicians, but their enthusiastic a cappella hymns are a majestic symphony to my love-starved heart. I drink it all in, eager to learn all I can.

I'm learning some awkward and confusing lessons. When I play with four-year-old William, I call him Willy, intending it as an affectionate nickname.

His eyes grow round, and he tells me quite seriously, "My name isn't Willy. It's William."

"But Willy is easier to say," I insist, "and it fits a boy your size."

Looking alarmed, the little boy purses his lips and shakes his head firmly, so I give in.

"Okay then, William," I say, and he smiles in relief. Later his father explains to me that the family doesn't use nicknames. Only four years old, William already knows his culture's taboo against nicknames. I file away the lesson, determined not to distress my little friend.

William teaches me another lesson when I teasingly hold him over the toilet and threaten to flush him. Thinking I'm serious, he kicks and screams in terror. Startled, I set him down, feeling like a brute as he sobs in relief. Like all children in this culture, he's been taught to accept whatever adults tell him as truth. His parents never tell their children about Santa Claus or the tooth fairy or anything that's not factual, so William takes my teasing at face value.

This new lifestyle offers order and predictability, which feels good after my years of chaos. The family and community bonds are strong, and I'm eager to earn their acceptance. My hosts graciously avoid pressuring me into immediate conformity with all their cultural quirks, although there's one thing: my long hair is too much for them. They quote Bible verses that indicate men's hair should be short. I tell them pictures of Jesus portray him with long hair, but they argue that the artists were mistaken since Jesus perfectly exemplified the Bible's teachings and would have kept his hair short.

Mr. Miller asks me often, "So when are you going to let me cut your hair?"

I brush him off, although his persistence is wearing me down. The family has been so loving and accommodating that I believe I owe them some token of gratitude.

One day I tell myself that the next time Mr. Miller asks, I'll let him cut off my prized ponytail.

That evening, as we're preparing for bed, he asks, "When are you going to let me cut your hair?"

"Right now," I say.

Mr. Miller is so used to my resistance that he continues with his usual argument.

"You know the Bible says it's a shame for a man to have long hair," he persists.

"Go ahead and cut it," I say again.

His face splits into a broad grin as he places a stool in the middle of the room, and like a waiter escorting a diner to his table, gestures for me to sit. He wraps an old sheet around me and stands beside me, scissors in one hand and electric clipper in the other. As the family crowds around to watch and grin, he's snipping away.

Feeling conspicuous and embarrassed, I tightly close my eyes. This is my first haircut in more than four years, and I don't like it. My mind drifts back to the haircut forced on me when I came back from Mexico. Mr. Miller is far gentler than the airport barber had been. My haircut at the airport represented anger and disappointment. This one represents new life.

Still, I groan when Mr. Miller cuts my ponytail and I hear it hit the floor. Soon the entire job is finished. I stare at my hair, pondering the history it represents. Countless episodes of drug use, aimless wandering, and hippie communes are now in the past.

> I stare at my hair, pondering the history it represents. Countless episodes of drug use, aimless wandering, and hippie communes are now in the past.

What will Gina think? I wonder. She's still in New Jersey, and although we've been writing letters and talking by phone a few times, she doesn't grasp all the changes happening in my life. How will she respond once we get back together? *Will she leave me? Will she become a Christian too?*

The next day I wrap the ponytail in paper and mail it to Gina. As I write "Ha ha ha" all over the package, I'm trying to imagine her reaction. Although I've lost a piece of myself, cutting my hair feels strangely freeing. It reminds me I'm leaving the old life behind and starting a new one.

One thing still bothers me. Although I know God has forgiven my sins, I can't forget what Peter told me the night we dropped Gina at the airport: "Someday, when you know the truth, you'll go back and pay for everything you stole."

Almost everything I own is either stolen or borrowed and never returned. Stealing and cheating were my way of life. It's really bothering me. It's time to right my past wrongs. Maybe God will help me.

> Stealing and cheating were my way of life. It's really bothering me. It's time to right my past wrongs.

* * * * *

After telling Peter and the Miller family my plans, I head out in my old green Ford. Since I've spent most of the past few years in Virginia and Georgia, I head there first. I make a list of people I've stolen from or wronged. One by one, I visit or send them letters, confessing my wrongs, asking forgiveness, and paying back what I owe.

Their responses vary. Some are puzzled and confused by my apologies, but most respond with kindness. Although some of my past deeds could have sent me to prison, no one presses charges. Everyone is gracious, and many are pleasantly surprised.

Regardless of how people are responding, I feel God smiling. Many times, before I make an apology, I'm afraid I'll meet angry people who'll demand consequences. Although I'm new to the Bible, God whispers to me the verse from James 2:13: "Mercy rejoices against judgment." I deserve judgment, and we all know it. I'm admitting to people my wrongs against them without making any excuses. Instead of receiving the harsh penalties of judgment I deserve, mercy instead is smiling.

For example, at Virginia Tech in Blacksburg, I had obtained a fake ID, lived in the dorm, and eaten in the cafeteria without paying. I find the right office and am sitting across the desk of an average-sized, athletic-looking man, probably in his forties. I make a full confession.

The man says, "You know we could press charges, right?"

"Yes, I understand," I respond. "Do what you need to do. I only want peace and a clear conscience."

"We won't press charges," he assures me. "Your confession is good enough."

I hand him a check for two hundred and fifty dollars and say, "I think this should cover what I stole from you."

"We can't take your money," he says with a kind smile, sliding the check back across the desk. "We don't have an account for this."

"It's not my money," I insist. "It's what I stole from you. Please take it."

He accepts the check, and I leave his office feeling lighter.

* * * * *

As I continue my restitution journey, I think about how impossible it felt when Peter told me I would need to make pay back everything I had stolen or borrowed. But now I'm doing it, with peace in my heart, and I sense God is with me.

As restitution depletes my meager savings, I'm wondering if I should keep going. Then a Christian friend, probably in his early twenties, approaches me in Blacksburg. He holds out his hand and gives me a warm, firm handshake.

"People all over town are talking about you," he says. "They say you're getting your life right, and I want to bless you for it." We enter a bank together, and he withdraws some money. To my surprise, he presses a folded stack of cash into my hand. Too embarrassed to count it, I shove it in my pocket.

Later, when I count the money, I'm shocked to find he gave me two hundred dollars! That's a lot of money in 1974, and I know God wants me to finish making restitution.

When I send letters to my parents, confessing what I stole from them and how I've disrespected them, Mom and Dad wonder if I'm clearing my conscience before taking my life. Despite their divorce

I drive to Atlanta, hoping to reconcile with Dad. This will be the scariest stop of all.

and strained relationship, this gets them talking to each other, trying to figure out what I'm up to.

I drive to Atlanta, hoping to reconcile with Dad. This will be the scariest stop of all. I call to let him know I'm coming and want to apologize to him.

My hands tremble as I knock on his front door. As I hear him unlatching the door, I brace myself for his familiar rejection and abuse.

Dad opens the door, and we stare at each other for a moment, each trying to read the other's expression. He extends a hand toward me, and when I reach to shake it, Dad pulls me close for a hug. Before I can recover from the shock, he astonishes me further by kissing me on the lips.

The church I'm attending has a practice of greeting each other with a "holy kiss" as described in the Bible, but I never expect this from Dad. Is he practicing an old Jewish custom? I don't know, but I feel accepted in that moment and deeply moved, like a tiny spark of hope that even this shattered relationship might yet be healed.

I follow Dad into the living room, sit on the couch, and face him in his rocking chair. It hurts to see how much he has aged.

"Dad, I'm sorry for all the trouble I caused you," I say gently. "I'm a Christian now."

There. I said it, I got the words out. I'm relieved.

Dad stares at me quizzically but doesn't immediately respond, so I continue. "I'm not rejecting my heritage, Dad. Jesus was a Jew, and I'm following him now. I've turned from my sins and want to live a different life. No more drugs, stealing, or lying. People from the church are helping me. I'm sorry for the way I treated you and Mom. I stole from you both, and I often lied. I disrespected you both."

"Phil, are you going crazy?" Dad asks, his brow furrowed in real concern.

"I'm not crazy, Dad. I'm trying to live for God now."

"I don't agree with Christianity," he says, slowly shaking his head. "But at least you're doing something good with your life. I can see you're going in a better direction than the way you were going."

Relief washes over me at his calm response. I expect Dad to shame and abuse me for leaving Judaism, but he's expressing peace with my decision. I never could figure him out.

While in Atlanta I contact Sears to make restitution for the pistol and other items I had stolen with Mike. They have no record of our theft, so I head to the police station. Since Mike and I were juveniles at the time, our records are sealed. Unable to pay anyone back, I accept God's forgiveness as a gift.

Of course, even when I'm able to repay, I still need God's undeserved forgiveness, but it helps when people express forgiveness. One of the most beautiful responses comes from an old farmer who owned a house near the farmhouse I had rented in Virginia. I send him a letter apologizing for breaking into his house and stealing a heater and some other stuff. I ask how much I should pay to make it right.

His misspelled and nearly illegible reply warms my heart:

Dear Philip,
All is forgiven. Don't let your consience bother you no more. You just keep on being a Christian.

> *Your friend,*
> *Leander*

* * * * *

On a later trip to see Mom in Miami, I visit the owner of the taxi company where Wally and I worked. My former boss appears suspicious of my intentions, and I notice he's keeping his right hand behind a manila folder he's holding. Is he concealing a gun?

"Do you remember the morning you asked if I used heroin and told me the FBI was watching me?" I ask him.

"Yeah, I remember."

"Well, I lied to you, and I want to apologize. I was using heroin at the time. I'm not using drugs anymore, and I'm trying to straighten up my life."

A big smile spreads across his face, and he lowers the folder to extend his hand. Either he wasn't holding a gun, or he quietly put it away.

"I'm sure it feels good to come clean," he says as he gives me a firm handshake. "Thanks for coming back and telling me. I'm glad you're straightening out your life."

Chapter 16

CROSSROADS

I always loved reading. Even at home, when all we had was the *National Enquirer, Reader's Digest,* and *True Confessions* magazines, I loved to read. Now I'm obsessed with reading the Bible. I can't get enough of its message; it's lighting me up inside. Hearing the Scriptures read in Hebrew in the synagogue didn't reach my heart, but now the *Bible* is speaking straight to my insides. Its truth makes sense of my life, and it grips me in ways no other book ever has.

My new church friends are sending me letters during my restitution trip—to the local post office wherever I happen to be—and each time I read their kind words and encouraging messages I long to return to their simple community. I want to change, and I believe they want to help me change. If I can fit into their culture, I'll finally have a place where I belong and am accepted.

But what about Gina? Will she take this radical step with me? I write her a long, heartfelt letter saying I'm a Christian now and thinking of joining the church in Tennessee. Will she consider becoming a Christian with me?

* * * * *

Gina flies from her parents' home in New Jersey and we meet in Blacksburg to discuss our future. We find a park, sit at a picnic table, and talk for hours.

"I've been offered a job managing an art gallery in New Mexico," she tells me. "You know how much I've wanted something like that."

We sit silently, contemplating the implications. If she accepts this job, we'll be going our separate ways, and I can't imagine living without her.

"On the other hand," Gina continues, "I wrote to one of my church friends in Tennessee and told her you were thinking about joining them. She wrote a beautiful letter back and said she hopes I'll become her sister in Christ. That touched me, and I think I'd like to have her as a sister."

Gina gazes thoughtfully at me for a moment, then continues. "Phil, I can tell you're different. You're not angry like you used to be."

"I feel different inside. And I want to live for God."

"What about Summertown?" Gina asks, referring to a large hippie commune we had earlier hoped to visit.

We fall silent again, pondering our options, and we only see two.

Should we join the old-fashioned country church in Tennessee and embrace their simple, stoic lifestyle? Or should we try to live for God in a hippie commune?

We think being Christians means accepting a rigid set of rules the church has set for us. As much as I'll need to change to join this Christian group, Gina will have to change more. The women wear long, solid-colored dark dresses and large bonnet-like coverings on their heads. They work long hours in their gardens, preserving food for their families, and sewing all their own clothes. Is Gina willing to do that?

In the Summertown commune, we can live close to nature, get high, and won't need to marry.

Still unsure of our final destination, we load our belongings into our old green Ford. With our trunk lid flapping, mismatched tires, and sagging ceiling, we head for Tennessee.

"I like the Mennonites," I muse, "and I think they care about us. But they won't let us stay together since we're not married. And we'll have to dress like them to join their church."

"And we'll have to stop playing music," Gina adds. The church allows only a cappella singing and believes listening to or playing musical instruments is sinful. Ever since Wally's melodies soothed my troubled spirit, music has played a vital role in my life. Can I really give up music to become one of them?

> Ever since Wally's melodies soothed my troubled spirit, music has played a vital role in my life. Can I really give up music to become one of them?

"At least the hippie commune would feel familiar," I suggest. "It's bigger than Lighthouse Ridge, but it could feel the same, and we could live together, play music, and keep getting high."

But then in my mind's eye I see the peaceful, orderly families sitting around the table and working together. Their highly structured world leaves no room for doubt, confusion, or chaos. Maybe their community would provide the stability I need.

As the Ford approaches the decision-making crossroad, we have to choose. Which way will we go? Will we join the Summertown hippie commune or the Mennonites? Our future hangs by a thread on one decision. If we're going to continue driving, we only have a few minutes left to make one of the most consequential decisions of our lives, one that could define our lives and family for decades—perhaps generations.

"Which way?" I ask Gina.

"I don't know," she shrugs. Gina dislikes making decisions.

"Come on," I say. "I'm driving, so you decide."

"I still don't know."

"Hurry up! You've got three-tenths of a mile to make up your mind."

Gina takes a deep breath, slowly exhales, and says, "Let's go to the Mennonites."

I sigh deeply and look at her. Now I imagine Gina and me and a few little ones gathered around the dining room table, smiling, singing, and praying.

"I think we made the right decision," I tell Gina as we head toward the church community.

Chapter 17

FINDING GOD AND MYSELF IN THE PIGPEN

Our decision made, Gina and I set to work creating our new identity as members of the Mennonite community. Since Gina's birth certificate has her given name as Mary (Gina was derived from her middle name, Virginia), our new friends insist on calling her Mary, a good biblical name. Gina protests at losing her identity, but women are required to submit without questioning, so her objections are swept aside. Although I've been called Phil for years, that's considered too casual, so I become Phillip.

Not only do we get new names, we also change our appearance to conform with the community's dress regulations. My hair is short, and I let my beard grow longer. I wear only solid-colored, long-sleeved shirts buttoned all the way up. My homemade trousers, either black or denim, are held up by black suspenders. Any time I go out in public, I wear a black hat as required by the church.

Gina, or Mary, as we now call her, looks like a born member of the community in her long somber dresses and thick white cap. Mary and I move into separate homes with two different church families, and living with them helps us learn their ways even more quickly.

Despite our willingness to embrace the oddities of this culture, it's not easy to join the church. Before they will baptize us, we have to attend what they call instruction class. It consists of many hours of learning their interpretation of biblical doctrines and memorizing the rules that regulate our lives.

This instruction period is also a test to see if we can live up to their written and unwritten standards. We're supposed to use this opportunity to cleanse ourselves from the accumulated stains of a lifetime as sinners. Attaining their definition of "separated from the world" is supposed to take the better part of a year. We learn to accept the endless rules not only as normal for Christians, but also good and desirable.

Church members' houses are not to have carpets or rugs on the floor. Only hardwood, linoleum, or some other simple floor surfaces keep us separated from the world. No light fixtures are permitted— only bare bulbs in white or ivory porcelain sockets. The walls are basically bare except for a few Bible verses. Anything more is considered tending toward pride and worldliness.

Labor-saving devices like dishwashers also are forbidden because the community is skeptical of progress and wants to preserve the simple life of an earlier era.

However, these folks use some modern inventions, like telephones and automobiles (although the cars have to be inexpensive and black), but they reject many other innovations. To someone who didn't grow up in the culture, the choices about what's allowed or banned appear arbitrary, but it makes perfect sense to those inside.

The church people emphasize hard work, and we're expected to earn our living by producing something tangible with our hands. Many church members are farmers, and even this traditional livelihood is regulated to prevent worldly temptations coming from wealth. Farmers aren't permitted to milk more than thirty-five cows. Tractors are to have less than sixty-five horsepower. Farmers aren't to possess a complete set of farm machinery to make it necessary to borrow from one another to encourage cooperation and community. Before members secure a loan from a brother or a bank, buy a car, or purchase property, the elders—and sometimes all the voting brothers over the age of 18—have to approve.

In a culture that emphasizes hard work and contentment, we're told that any form of entertainment is incompatible with separation from the world, so we have no television, radio, or other electronics.

Despite the strict rules, I'm excited about my new life and throw myself wholeheartedly into becoming the best Christian I can. With my limited understanding, I think Christianity means Mennonite. I want to live for God now, and these people seem to have it figured out to the smallest detail, so I don't hold back. Enthusiastically, I wear the old-fashioned clothing, paint my green Ford black, give up playing music, and do everything else according to their interpretations of the Bible.

I'm also searching for work that meets the church's requirement of working with my hands. I take any odd jobs I can find, from farm labor to truck farming to carpentry and masonry. Most jobs are paying two or three dollars an hour.

I'm thrilled when I'm hired as a laborer for six dollars an hour at a Housing and Urban Development housing project. After a few weeks, they offer me ten dollars an hour to be a site engineer, and I work hard at it. I buy a book called *Site Engineering* from a thrift store for a dollar, and study it diligently, even purchasing one of the first trigonometry calculators to help calculate the math I need. Mary studied trigonometry in college, so she helps me, but the complex math makes my head spin.

Most of these jobs drive me to despair because I'm out of my element using so much complicated math. What now?

Then I think about woodworking. My first experience working with wood had been Mr. Klehm's high school woodworking shop class. I remember my deep satisfaction from building a walnut desk and nightstand under his guidance. Can I experience that fulfillment again through woodworking?

I'm going to try. I still own a band saw and drill press from my days making soapstone marijuana pipes back in Virginia. I set up these tools, and a few more that I borrow, in a neighbor's 12-foot square pigpen. That's right: a pigpen. The barn housed pigs until the farmer moved them into another part of the barn and let me use the space for woodworking. Despite the unusual setting and cramped quarters, I'm immediately in my element.

Using walnut, cherry, and cedar lumber I handpick from local sawmills, I build fancy porch swings. In one day, I can build a four- or five-foot swing that sells for twenty dollars. The price includes all the hardware, a coat of varnish, and even installation. I find building and hanging a swing a satisfying day's work. A more complex but equally satisfying project is crafting multi-unit purple martin birdhouses I sell for forty-five dollars.

> My mind is still haunted by darkness, but the darkness always retreats when I lose myself in crafting something beautiful from wood.

Something in me comes to life when I turn raw wood into tangible things people value and enjoy. My mind is still haunted by darkness, but the darkness always retreats when I lose myself in crafting something beautiful from wood.

With a satisfying occupation that meets the church's approval, I can turn my attention to the complicated task of joining the church with Mary. After almost a year of instruction class and strict adherence to the rules, we're considered worthy of church membership. After we repeat some vows, the bishop pours a small amount of water on our heads and baptizes us into their church.

I think we've arrived at last, but nothing is ever that easy.

Mary and I learn that in addition to explicit rules, this church, like many religious groups, has unspoken norms and taboos difficult for an outsider to detect. Very few people from the "outside" succeed in joining their strict, rules-centered churches, and even fewer stay permanently.

Thus, when "Phillip and Mary" manage to keep all their rules, we become special trophies. We're validating their understanding of Christianity. They claim to be different from and better than the world, and they feel validated by converting dirty sinners like Mary and me and making us look and act like them.

Another church mandate involves my relationship with Mary. Since we had lived together but weren't married, the leaders tell us we either have to marry each other or remain single for the rest of our lives. They're pleased that we've joined their church, but their acceptance has limits. We're damaged, unworthy of marrying into any of the families we admire so much.

Thus, when "Phillip and Mary" manage to keep all their rules, we become special trophies. We're validating their understanding of Christianity.

Although we've been in love at times during our relationship, Mary and I also experience way too much turbulence and conflict. My periodic episodes of rage and our constant drug use have left us both damaged. On a few occasions I physically assaulted her during an argument. That was before we came to this church, of course, but the pain of those experiences remains. By the time we finish the trial period and are baptized, we don't like each other anymore. Yet we're conflicted because in this new world, we think we only have each other. We feel trapped and powerless to change our bizarre circumstances.

Because of my insecurity, I'm terrified of living alone and tell Mary we should get married rather than spend the rest of our lives alone. As she wrestles with that decision, the church leaders and I pressure her with, "The Bible says a woman must submit to the man." Never mind that we're not married; they and I still play the submission card to pressure Mary into complying.

The elders suggest that if Mary doesn't marry me, she can work in a nursing home in Canada that's staffed by workers from churches like ours. Having grown up in Louisiana, Mary hates winters and isn't interested in Canada.

At last, driven by guilt, shame, and pressure to submit, she agrees to marry me. We're not in love, and she doesn't get to experience a memorable proposal, but we're engaged.

We plan our wedding for February of 1976.

Chapter 18

THEY WOULDN'T EVEN LET ME SAY GOODBYE

The September before our wedding, I call Mom to let her know we've set the date.

"Mary and I want to invite both you and Dad to the wedding if you promise not to fight," I say.

"I can't make that promise," Mom insists. "If an argument starts, we're going to fight."

Although I beg her to commit to keeping our wedding peaceful, she refuses to promise.

"Ask your father," Mom snaps at me. Although I'm now reconciled with Dad and treasure the memory of his hug and kiss, he's still explosive, likely to erupt without provocation, and I feel helpless. Around midnight Mom and I end the conversation, and I go to bed frustrated.

The next night, a sharp knock on my bedroom door startles me awake.

"Phone for you," a sleepy voice says.

I shuffle into the kitchen and pick up the phone. It's Mom.

"Phil, your father's dead."

"What happened?" I whisper hoarsely.

"He was playing with a gun, showing off to some of his employees. No one is sure how or why it happened, but he shot himself in the head."

"When did this happen?" I ask.

"About five this afternoon."

My mind is reeling. Dad has been dead seven hours, and no one thought to let me know until now? Although our relationship has always been stormy and furious, the news of his death still shatters me. No longer can I cling to the hope that we'll grow closer or understand each other. Our story is over now, and nothing can change that.

Mr. Miller is now standing in the kitchen as Mom promises to call later with funeral details.

"What happened?" he asks as I softly return the phone to its cradle.

"My father's dead," I manage to say.

"Oh," he replies without emotion, then turns and shuffles back to bed.

I head to bed also, but I can't sleep. My dad's dead! My father, whom I loved and feared and hated and ran from—he's dead! How is this possible?

Feeling desperate, I call the bishop at 1:30 am to ask if I can come over and talk.

"Of course, come right over," he says, and his kind voice gives me a ray of hope.

As I drive, waves of darkness engulf me. I try to pray, but my thoughts are an endless, despairing scream. The cool, clear night and twinkling stars should offer me comfort, but I'm too numb. The five miles to the bishop's house seem long. I knock on the door. He's dressed and waiting, holding the door open for me.

I step inside the doorway and say, "My father's dead."

"Oh, Phillip, I'm sorry!" Compassion glistens in his eyes.

I feel far away. Dad lived a wild life. I've mentally rehearsed his death many times. Now here it is, and I don't know how to act. Dad's dead. I need some way to deny it. *Maybe Mom just said the words,* I tell myself, *but he's really alive . . . No, he's dead. He's really dead. My own father's dead. How does a person act when his father dies?*

The bishop and I talk awhile, and then we kneel for a long time. My mind tosses and tumbles, but I'm too tormented to pray.

I try desperately to conjure some happy memories, but I can't recall any. Then I remember my recent visit with Dad and his welcome hug and kiss. I desperately cling to that one happy memory.

The bishop and I stay up all night. Just before dawn I drive to the deacon's house where Mary is staying. She's sitting on a wooden chair in the kitchen.

"My father's dead," is all I can say.

Tears trickle down her cheeks.

The deacon's wife, shocked to see me talking to Mary without their consent, sternly snaps, "What are you doing here?"

"His father's dead," her husband gently explains, reassuring her that we're not acting inappropriately.

But because of their strict courtship rules, Mary and I remain stiffly apart, unable to comfort each other in our grief.

* * * * *

A few days later, several people from the church drive to Atlanta with Mary and me for Dad's funeral. Our old-fashioned clothes appear out of place at a liberal Jewish funeral, but I don't care.

We step into the room where Dad is. I ask the others to give me a few minutes alone with him. The family respectfully files out, and I ask Mary to remain with me.

Dad looks as handsome as always. His hair and mustache are neatly trimmed. He wears an expensive-looking suit and tie. His hands, neatly folded over his stomach, are slightly raised in the air, probably due to rigor mortis. I search for the bullet hole in his head, but it's apparently been skillfully patched with skin-colored wax.

I always thought death happened to other people. Uncle Bert and Grandpa Jim died, Scotty accidentally killed himself, and my best

This is my dad, and he's dead. Dad, whom I feared, ran away from, rebelled against, and loved so much because he's the only father I've ever had. He's part of me.

friend Wally had been murdered. But that was always *someone else*. This is different. This is my dad, and he's dead. Dad, whom I feared, ran away from, rebelled against, and loved so much because he's the only father I've ever had. He's part of me.

A strange sensation engulfs me. Seeing Dad in the coffin, I imagine myself dead.

Mary kneels next to me, and we try to pray, but our prayers feel awkward and meaningless.

I hear clamoring in the background. Loud stomping on the wooden floor. Shouting voices. Dad's second wife and my grandmother, Dad's mother, are fighting, shoving, and punching. Then Mom jumps into the fray. More fighting, shouting, pushing, running. Suddenly it stops! All is silent.

* * * * *

The next morning, I call the funeral home to confirm the funeral starts at 10 o'clock.

"No, it starts at 9:30."

It's almost 9:30 already. We won't make it on time.

"But I'm his son!" I nearly shout. "I'm supposed to be a pallbearer!"

"Sorry. We can't wait for you."

We skip the funeral service and head straight to the cemetery, but we get lost on the way. As we enter the cemetery, my family is leaving.

My sister rolls down the back window of the black limousine and says, "You're too late. It's over."

It's over! Mary and I park the car and climb the hill to Dad's grave. The earth is marked with a fresh dirt mound and a few scattered flowers. A floral arrangement, propped by the grave, has a picture of a clock stopped at five minutes till twelve. I wonder, *Is it five minutes till death for me or someone I know?*

Hot tears roll down my cheeks. Life is so unfair!

"Dad, I'm sorry. They wouldn't even let me say goodbye."

* * * * *

Back in Tennessee, when I enter the kitchen where I had taken Mom's phone call a few days before, the tears start to flow. I hurry outside and sink into a chair on the side porch.

As I'm weeping uncontrollably, Mr. Miller comes out and silently stares at me.

"What's the matter with you?" His voice is cool and even.

"My father died." I look up, searching his face for understanding and compassion.

"Oh," he says flatly and walks away, as he had the night Mom called about Dad's death. It's adding up now: these people disapprove of strong emotions. We must accept whatever happens as God's will. Strong emotions come from our old sinful self, which must be suppressed. I thought my dad's death would be an exception. It isn't.

Everything inside me shuts down. I want to release the pain of my sorrow, but that would lead to disapproval and rejection. My pain and stormy emotions aren't welcome here. As a loyal church member, I've separated myself from my family and friends because they're supposed to be heathen sinners. Drugs, music, sex, and primal screaming are also forbidden now, so I have no release.

And now my host's reaction shows that even tears aren't acceptable for a devout Christian.

So I shut down inside and buy into the whole thing with black hats, black cars, and black suspenders. I do my best to look and act like a good church member, and that's enough.

As I've done since childhood, once again I'm grieving and raging inside.

Chapter 19

NEWLYWEDS

With my beginner's knowledge of the Bible, I accept our church's rigid interpretation of Christianity as the only right one. Mary's nominally Protestant upbringing has given her some understanding of Christianity, but she doesn't know the Bible well. She's skeptical of needing so many detailed rules, but our leaders seem to have a Bible verse or doctrinal explanation for everything. Mary reasons that since they know the Bible better than us, their version of Christianity must be correct.

Despite our commitment to be loyal church members, we're mostly miserable. Their preaching demands levels of perfection we can't measure up to no matter how hard we try. Where is the simple joy I experienced when I met God in the woods? I'm drowning in my inability to measure up to this complicated set of spoken and unspoken rules.

Sometimes I express my confusion, asking questions like, "Why was I happier when I was a hippie than I am now?"

My honest questions provoke harsh reactions from the leaders, who sternly warn me to stop talking like that or I'll be in serious trouble. Their way is best, and questioning them is labeled as rebellion. Thus, I decide I'm miserable because God is punishing me for my past sins. So I try even harder to live a holy life. Maybe someday I'll earn my way out of this heavy retribution and into God's favor.

> I decide I'm miserable because God is punishing me for my past sins. So I try even harder to live a holy life.

* * * * *

On February 3, 1976, our wedding day, we look like lifelong Mennonites. A large head covering conceals Mary's strawberry blonde hair. Her oversized gray dress hangs loosely, nearly to the tops of her sturdy black shoes.

I'm wearing a black suit without lapels, buttoned all the way up, Catholic priest style. On my head is a black derby hat that's supposed to identify me as separated from the world. My heart is frozen; I'm stuck somewhere deep inside my head. I'm unable to look anyone in the eye. The night before our wedding, a blizzard hits the mountain where we live, preventing several people from attending. The barren, frozen, muddy conditions of the storm mirror our cold hearts and confused minds.

A warm sun greets the next day, melting most of the snow away. Daffodils are popping up everywhere, whispering to Mary's heart, *Everything will be okay.*

Around one hundred church people and a handful of our family members fill the old church meeting house. Two of the ministers each preach lengthy sermons. The congregation sings a few songs. My mom, brother, and sister are there, along with Mary's dad, mom, and two sisters. I'm sure they feel as strange and out of place as they appear.

Mary and I are sitting in the front of the building, on opposite sides of the aisle, backs to the congregation, facing the ministers. After the sermons the bishop stands and addresses Mary and me, "If you still desire holy matrimony, please rise to your feet."

We stand beside each other, stiff and unsmiling, careful not to touch each other's hands, while the bishop reads our wedding vows. We respond with "I do." He pronounces us man and wife, and then Mary and I solemnly shake hands with each other.

His declaration suddenly hits me like a judge slamming his gavel down, handing a life sentence to a condemned prisoner. I'm sure God is punishing me for my past sins by condemning me to live with a woman who doesn't want me.

The deacon's family hosts the reception and wedding meal for our guests at their house. We eat little sandwiches and potato casserole, with cake and fruit for dessert. It's quite frugal and simple, just like everything else we do in our community.

The deacon hands Mary's dad a detailed bill—including a few cents for the salt—for the food served at the reception. The total comes to a forty-seven dollars and some cents, so my new father-in-law hands him fifty dollars and tells him to keep the change.

Legally married now, Mary and I settle down to behaving like good church members. We bicker as much as ever, but now we're hiding it behind a pious image of "love at home." Even we believe the lie that we have a good marriage. Our newlywed experience is a strange mix of pleasure in the simple lifestyle and exhaustion from our efforts to appease an angry and demanding God.

Our house is small and simple, built in the 1940s from rough sawn lumber. We lack indoor plumbing, so we use an outhouse 200 feet from the house and haul our water inside from a well in the yard. A woodstove provides heat for warmth, cooking, and canning.

We can't afford groceries, so we raise our food in a large garden and can it on the wood cookstove in used canning jars we've purchased at yard sales and flea markets. We sterilize the jars and use new lids. Meat is a luxury we have when a farmer gives us a lame cow, which we butcher and store in the deep freezer Mary's parents gave us as a wedding present. Sometimes the local grocery store sells us cow heart, tongue, liver, and soup bones or chicken gizzards for 25 cents a pound.

Even paying the fifteen-dollar monthly rent or the four-dollar electric bill is a struggle.

Our bedroom is in the attic, and the siding on the back upper wall has rotted away. Sometimes in winter we wake up with snow on our bed. When hard thunderstorms hit, the noise on the tin roof is louder than any racket I've ever heard. Scared, I slip out of bed and drop to my knees, wondering if the world is coming to an end.

As small as our house is, I claim half of it for my woodworking shop. With money almost nonexistent, buying tools is out of the question. I often have to make my own tools, borrow them, or repurpose old ones. I build a large twelve-foot sander from rough lumber, purchasing used sanding belts for a dollar apiece from the local handle factory. While it speeds up the woodworking process, it spreads sawdust throughout the house. Mary has to wash dishes before as well as after we eat.

Despite the dust and noise, I'm finding tranquility and satisfaction in my craft. Through trial and error, I design a rocking baby cradle with a wooden canopy. Mary cuts a foam mattress to fit it, sews flannel sheets, and hand sews a pretty little quilt and bumper pad. Creating things with my new bride is a wonderful experience, and it feels good. We sell the finished cradles for one hundred dollars each, which feels like a fortune.

Encouraged by this success, I ask the local lumber yard if I can select the best pine boards. I improve the design of each new cradle until the rockers rock perfectly.

I build wooden toy trucks large and sturdy enough for a child to ride. They bring smiles to children and parents alike. I purchase galvanized roller skate wheels in bulk, using roofing nails for headlights. Mary paints the details: windshield, wipers, side doors, and the family name and occupation if they want it personalized.

My skills are improving, and I'm becoming more confident in my work. The days pass quickly. Working with wood takes my mind off myself, and for the first time in my life I feel useful. It's deeply satisfying that people acknowledge my skills at creating a cradle, birdhouse, or toy truck. The profits are small, but our lifestyle is simple, and I feel well compensated as I create things with my hands that make people happy.

Despite recurring bouts of dark depression, woodworking is the therapy that brings my soul rest. But while manual labor and building beautiful things invigorate and fulfill me, church life is becoming a tangled knot of confusion. Still determined to please God, I absorb the heavy-handed legalism as the only path to God's favor. Like a typical proselyte, I've become obsessively committed to keeping the rules and policing others even more than my fellow church members who were born into this culture.

My shoulders slump in weary resignation. "Brothers, I'm sorry," I say. "I promise to do better."

The burden of learning and keeping endless rules has become too heavy. God seems even more demanding than my dad had been.

However, despite my best efforts, I'm constantly getting into trouble. Sometimes I'm "wrong" about some detail of my clothes or hat. Other times, Mary attracts criticism for similarly obscure reasons of not appearing separate enough from the world.

For example, while enjoying a Sunday lunch at our friends' house, I briefly mention my work. The next day, two church leaders pay me a visit. I dread visits from our leaders because this usually means I've broken some rule and displeased God. Sure enough, the pastor says, "By talking about business on Sunday, you're not keeping the Sabbath."

My shoulders slump in weary resignation. "Brothers, I'm sorry," I say. "I promise to do better."

The burden of learning and keeping endless rules has become too heavy. God seems even more demanding than my dad had been. No matter how hard I try, I can't measure up, but I assume my spiritual leaders are Bible experts who know what God requires, so I'm plodding through my inner darkness, hoping the light comes soon. The joy I first experienced when God met me in the woods has been lost in a dark maze of rules and heavy religious demands. It's the only Christianity I know. Many times I'm driving down the road in my car, yelling, making up words I don't understand, and trying to connect with a God who's too far away to hear me.

Mary is doing better than me with it all. She has great social skills and quickly adapts to the homesteading skills needed for our new life. She learns to plant and tend a big garden, and she cans or freezes the food we raise ourselves or purchase from local farmers.

I'm torn between two forces: I'm pleased at Mary's unruffled adaptability, but I'm resentful that she's more accepted than I am in our community.

She appears to have her act together, so I'm as surprised as anyone when Mary experiences a profound change.

It begins as we're driving with a couple from our church to Chattanooga, hoping to convert some of our former hippie friends who fled from Lighthouse Ridge after one of the members was murdered one night.

On the way to Chattanooga, Mary shocks herself and me when she says, "I feel like a hypocrite, going to witness to our friends about a peace and joy that I don't even have."

I look at my wife, dumbfounded. How can she doubt her salvation? Hadn't she dutifully accepted everything we were taught during instruction class? Hadn't she proven herself and been rewarded with baptism into the church? Doesn't she dress simply while upholding all the church's rules? How can she *not* be a Christian?

The woman traveling with us perceives something is wrong. "I don't want to cause you unnecessary turmoil," she tells Mary. "But do you really know if you've been saved? Do you feel God calling you to himself? He'll show you the truth about your heart if you ask him."

Mary nods thoughtfully. "I do feel God drawing me. I don't want to settle for anything less than the truth."

Her friend's face lights up as she explains, "I remember when it happened to me. Everything changed when I was converted, and I felt fresh and new inside."

I can't contain myself and burst out, "But we're not supposed to go by our feelings! We're supposed to walk by faith. Mary, you dress modestly. You obey all the church's rules. You're submissive to your husband. Of course you're a Christian!"

Our friend smiles gently but shakes her head slightly. "I don't want to contradict you or presume to teach you, but I'm telling you what God has done for me. He changed me! I'm a new person!"

I'm getting rattled by her boldness. We expect women to be meek and quiet, not questioning men, but this woman doesn't hold back. Her face glows as she speaks, and I see spiritual hunger in Mary's face as she listens intently.

After we're home, I tell Mary, "That was weird. I've never heard anyone from church talk like that, and especially not a woman! She was out of her place."

"I want what she has," my wife says simply.

A few days later, Mary says, "I need time alone to think. I'm going for a walk."

When she returns, I can see something has happened to her. She has a contented glow. Too afraid to say anything, I go about my life. Mary is spontaneously singing as she performs her endless tasks, and her face glows with inner light. Even the drab dress and oversized head covering she wears don't diminish her radiant inner beauty.

That day when Mary took a walk in the woods, she encountered God, and she was changed.

It's obvious she's been transformed, but I'm scared to ask her about it. If she sees that experience as her conversion, where does that leave me? I know my prayer in the woods transformed me too, but that moment has long since faded into a fog of confusion. The unconditional love and acceptance I felt from God the day I met Jesus have been slowly replaced by an endless struggle to be good enough to earn the church's acceptance.

It's obvious she's been transformed, but I'm scared to ask her about it. If she sees that experience as her conversion, where does that leave me?

I've become critical and judgmental toward anyone who doesn't uphold our precise set of rules. Not only do I condemn all mainstream Protestant churches, I—along with my churchmates—am equally harsh in my judgment of other conservative Mennonites whose rules differ even slightly from ours. For example, our church allows push-button phones. A church we closely fellowship with allows only rotary phones and criticizes our church for our stance. One church requires all men to grow beards. Another church requires men to be clean-shaven. I don't stop to ask myself, "If churches want to differ over these details of living, why must they criticize and preach against churches that differ from them?"

Instead, I believe anyone who doesn't believe or practice just like us must be on the way to hell. And I openly drive my beliefs hard against anyone who's not like us.

Not surprisingly, I'm miserable!

Chapter 20

OUTCAST

Twice a year, our church observes communion. The weeks leading up to the communion service make everyone crazy anxious. A week or two before communion the elders conduct a gathering they call a council meeting. In it they meet privately with each church member to determine whether they're worthy to take communion. Anyone judged guilty of sin or rule-breaking during the previous six months faces public rebuke and gets banned from participating in the Lord's Supper.

It's a frantic frenzy of church members visiting one another to accuse each other of wrongdoing or rule-breaking. The sacrament of communion—intended to commemorate God's gracious gift of forgiveness and grace through Jesus' death and resurrection—has become more of a witch hunt as members search for ways to accuse one another of unworthiness to take communion which could defile the rest of us.

As the dreaded council meeting approaches, Mary's conversion has become an extensive controversy. Other women in the church who have observed the radical change in Mary's spirit question their own salvation. The leaders accuse Mary of needlessly upsetting these women. In the past, compliant submission has been enough to assure members of their spiritual good standing. This "doubt" that Mary is creating has caused turmoil in practically every household.

To complicate things even more, the deacon—yes, the one who hosted our wedding—accuses me of forcing Mary into a false conversion. For more than an hour, he relentlessly pounds on me verbally.

A few days before the council meeting, Mary and I are invited to dinner at the house of the woman who challenged Mary to question her salvation. This woman and her family exemplify our bishop's belief in simple living. In fact, their house is downright primitive, a cement block structure originally intended as a barn. As the husband and I chat in the makeshift living room while our wives talk in the kitchen, the children play with homemade wooden blocks on the concrete floor.

My friend is unusually quiet. Breaking the silence at last, he says, "Phillip, my wife and I believe there are only four people in church who are real Christians."

"Only four?" I asked nervously. "Who?"

He counts them off on his fingers: his wife, himself, his mother-in-law (the motherly lady who welcomed me into her family when I first joined the community), and Mary, my wife.

My heart drops like a rock when I realize I'm excluded. He doesn't believe I'm a true believer? Didn't God save me at Lighthouse Ridge? And haven't I made all my restitution? Apparently, that's not enough. Mary has made it on the "saved list" while I haven't. We'll be separated for eternity unless I figure out how to become a real Christian like her.

I sit silently, trying to hide the war raging in my soul.

✳ ✳ ✳ ✳ ✳

Still haunted and confused a few weeks later, I descend the stairs to the church's basement where the council meeting has started. In addition to the usual "As far as I know, I have peace with God and man" statement we all make, I tell the preachers about my friend's claim that only four church members are real Christians. Unaware of the damage that's about to be unleashed by what I've just exposed, I leave the meeting hoping I've been judged worthy to take communion.

The leaders move swiftly to suppress this perceived threat against their authority. Within days, they excommunicate three of the four "real Christians," with only Mary escaping church discipline. She's so obviously changed by her conversion that, I suspect, they can't deny her experience and thus leave her alone. The reason given for excommunicating the other three is heresy.

> Excommunication includes shunning, so the three heretics will be completely ignored until they demonstrate enough repentance to be reinstated.

Excommunication includes shunning, so the three heretics will be completely ignored until they demonstrate enough repentance to be reinstated. If church members socialize, conduct business, or even eat with the erring ones, they too will be excommunicated—shunned!

I've endured rejection all my life, but this shunning elevates things to a new level. It's an organized, systematic act of rejection meant to isolate the offender until he or she has earned restoration back into the church.

I've worked so hard to earn acceptance in this church, but now my progress feels fragile. When will I misstep and find myself outside the church, shunned by these people whom I believe are God's only saved ones?

In the meantime, an even greater turmoil surfaces in the church.

Let me go back to how the church started. Concerned about the prosperous Mennonites in Ohio becoming slaves to their wealth, two Mennonite brothers from Ohio move in the 1960s to one of the poorest counties in Tennessee, determined to live a simpler life—their definition of how Christians must live. For thirty-five dollars an acre, they buy several hundred acres of woodland and a bulldozer. They clear land and build houses and a church meeting house. Their idea is for everyone to live on small "Old McDonald" farms, raising most of their food and butchering livestock for meat.

By contrast, several families move in from Maryland, Pennsylvania, and Ohio to take advantage of the cheap land and create large farming operations they can divide among their growing families and keep their children nearby.

Our beloved bishop, who taught me to deeply study the Bible and pray sincerely, is now ordaining new leaders, not from those who intensely love the Word of God, but those who side with him in making and enforcing tighter rules intended to force church members to keep their operations small.

After hundreds of hours of late night meetings and open conflicts during Sunday Bible studies at the church, the church finally splits. Mary and I remain with the original group. More than a dozen families move away to start another church 50 miles away. Sadly, families divide—brothers, parents, children, and even a marriage—with members joining opposing groups.

Imagine several farmers selling off large parcels of land in a small, rural community. Land prices drop. Imagine these same farmers buying large parcels of land in another small, rural community. Land prices skyrocket! Now imagine they're doing all this with borrowed money, it's 1980, and mortgage rates are 18 percent!

Hundreds of thousands of dollars evaporate in a bitter church split that decimates families, people's hard-earned net worth, and what Mary and I thought was the beautiful church we had been searching for.

Although the new church keeps many of the same rules, the two groups view each other with contempt and refuse to fellowship with anyone who chooses to affiliate with the other side.

In reality, the only difference between the two groups is business philosophy, which could be resolved if the love of Christ were large enough in their hearts. Both sides believe in modest and old-fashioned clothing, women's head coverings, not participating in war, rejecting divorce and remarriage, separating from the world, and many other good things. Despite sharing most of the same beliefs, the small difference is enough to split the church and divide families.

Some accuse *me* of causing the split as the troublemaker who stirs up church problems. The despair I feel at this accusation is all too familiar. This is how I felt when Mom and Dad fought—trapped in the middle, wondering what was wrong with me and how I could cause so much trouble. How is this happening again?

* * * * *

In the midst of all this, I'm trying to figure out how to be a godly dad. In 1977, our first son, Noah, is born. Over the next thirteen and a half years, eight more children are born into our family, a total of five sons and four daughters.

I don't know how to be a father. Despite all my religious efforts, I'm becoming the ill-tempered father my dad had been, only I'm not living in adultery or using drugs or alcohol. Instead of bringing me joy, parenting terrifies me. All my life I've been labeled a failure. Dad called me a failure, as did my teachers, employers, fellow hippies, and now the church! They all have the same message: I don't measure up. I'm not good enough. I'm a failure. Naturally, I'll be a failure as a father too, and I don't know how I'll survive that.

* * * * *

In 1984, I meet my Judgment Day. I believe it starts when I confide in a minister about my deepening depression.

I ask him the questions I've asked many times before: "Why was I happier when I was a hippie than I am now?" And, "Why does the

Bible call the Gospel 'good news'? My life should be joyful, but I'm miserable."

He says some vague things meant to set me straight, but his words don't do anything for me.

He rebukes me. "Phillip, you say you want answers, but whenever someone tries to help, you think you know better and refuse to listen!"

One dark autumn evening, I'm summoned to the church meeting house for a brothers' meeting about "Brother Phillip's situation." The pastors are at their wits' end, especially with my chronic depression. They can't understand or fix it, so they say I'm proud, and that they're here to discuss what to do with me.

I've been a church member for about eight years. I've changed on the outside, but I'm empty inside. Keeping rules isn't fixing me. I'm too tired and wounded to hold up a heavy Christian front. My leaders believe the emotional pain I carry from Dad's abuse, my past drug use, and Dad's sudden death are coming from my sinful nature. They want me to stuff my pain, but I don't know how, so they label my depression pride and rebellion.

Despair billows over me as I sit in the meeting, listening to my brothers discuss my fate. The church leaders go downstairs. The lay members follow, one by one, to cast their vote on my future.

After about an hour, they've finished voting. The bishop returns. He bishop stands squarely behind the pulpit while the two other ministers take seats, flanking him on the left and right. None of them look at me. I scan their faces, but I can't read their blank expressions.

The clears his throat. Then he says, soberly, "The unanimous counsel of the brethren is to excommunicate Phillip and turn him over to Satan."

Then, looking straight at me, he says, "May God have mercy on your soul."

While appearing calm on the outside, waves of hot emotion sweep over me as I internalize his words. Have I sinned so grievously against God that they must thrust me out of the church and God's kingdom?

I hear only scattered phrases as the bishop closes the meeting . . .

" . . . treat him as a heathen and a publican."

" . . . we will not eat or commune with Phillip, nor have social fellowship, nor do any business with him."

The next day, I'm paralyzed in my bed until almost noon while the rest of the family goes about the usual business of living. The older children go to school, and Mary tends to her household duties.

I hear the words echo inside: "Pride. You have too much pride."

"God," I groan, "teach me. If I'm proud, then I need humility. How do I get it?"

I flip through the Bible, and find this in 1 John 2:16: "For all that is in the world, the lust of the flesh, and the lust of the eyes, and the pride of life, is not of the Father, but is of the world."

"For all that is in the world, the lust of the flesh, and the lust of the eyes, and the pride of life, is not of the Father, but is of the world."

I reflect on what the church teaches about pride. Pride is having too many cows, a car that's too new or not painted black, or brightly colored clothing and home furnishings. I think about my woodworking. Is making nice furniture pride? Should I stop trying to get such a smooth finish on the pieces I make? Is this the pride they're punishing me for?

I contemplate this for days, praying and begging God to help me. Going to church is painful. Instead of giving me the customary kiss of peace and a warm handshake, the men stiff-arm me and give me cold, hard stares.

The church people treat me as though I don't exist. I conclude I'm a godless criminal. I live in a community surrounded by church members, yet months pass without any of them talking to me. If they see me coming, they create a wide space and avoid me. They won't eat with me. They won't help me except in an emergency. They won't do business with me. I'm not allowed to attend social events except church services.

For example, it's a bright sunny Monday. Curtis comes to see me. He gives me a stiff handshake and cold stare. "I hope you see your sin and come around someday."

Long, silent pause . . .

"I'll be back in a few days," he says, then leaves.

About a week later, Curtis returns. He offers another cold stare and stiff handshake.

"Any questions?" he asks.

"I don't understand what's happening here," I reply.

Long pause . . .

"I just wondered if you had any questions." He turns and leaves.

If another church member is even suspected of socializing or doing business with me, they'll be interrogated and likely be excommunicated as well.

I'm convinced our church is God's chosen people, and everyone else around us is lost and going to hell.

Because of that I feel two things: first, it's like I'm kneeling and begging for mercy while repeatedly getting punched in the face.

Second, it's like my brethren have tossed me overboard into shark-infested waters, leaving me to be devoured by the wicked world outside.

* * * * *

Still desperate, I fly to Miami to visit my mother and grandmother. The previous few days in Tennessee have been stormy with rain. As the plane ascends above the clouds, I gaze out the window at a clear blue sky above a beautiful, flaming, red and white sunset. As I absorb the glorious scene, I tell myself: *It doesn't matter what I must endure and how stormy my life will be. If I keep moving toward God, my sunset will be glorious.*

> I return to
> Tennessee, and
> I'm so lonely and
> desolate I tell
> myself I'm going
> to do whatever it
> takes to get back
> into the church.

I seek comfort from Mom and Grandma Mary, but my flavor of pain is too foreign for them. I take long walks along the Miami streets and beaches. One day I wander into a Christian bookstore and purchase a key ring with an oval-shaped silver tab that reads: "They that wait upon the Lord shall renew their strength."

For many months, I'll be clinging to the words on that small silver tab as my only hope. I return to Tennessee, and I'm so lonely and desolate I tell myself I'm going to do whatever it takes to get back into the church. I pray. I read the Bible. I try to figure out how I've offended people. I make apologies where I can.

* * * * *

After a few months, the ministers meet and tell me the brethren have voted and agreed to lift the shunning and put me on "proving," which is their form of probation.

I barely hear the proving part because I'm so elated that I'm at least partly accepted now! They still don't extend the kiss of peace, but at least I can attend social functions and eat with everyone else. I can come to community workdays! My spirit feels light.

In the back of my mind, I know the proving period will likely last six months or more, and I'm only a slight notch above slipping back into shunning. I'm walking a tightrope because proving means just that—proving! Everyone stands on the sidelines, watching, waiting for me to either measure up or fail.

I'm trying hard not to be controversial. I want everyone to see I've changed, that I'm now humble instead of proud.

My bouts with depression are lightening. I feel more loved and accepted by the church. My woodworking business is prospering, and now I can work again with other church members.

Life is getting somewhat better . . . but deep down I know I'm the same inside.

One day I meet a neighbor I hung out with at the local beer joint before I met Jesus. He says, "Let's get together sometime."

I reply, "I don't know. I've changed now."

His response: "You've changed on the outside. You're still the same on the inside."

What does he know that I don't know?

I'm trying to convince the church I'm different. But not much inside me has changed. I'm doing the best I can.

Chapter 21

THE HEART OF A CRAFTSMAN

It's 1982. Woodworking provides one of the few bright spots in my life. Darkness, despair, and depression fill my life, but when I explore the beauty in wood, I feel something close to happiness.

However, after five years of using half of our tiny 24 x 24 house as my shop, the situation is no longer sustainable. Because we live on a gravel road and our house doesn't have any insulation, it's perpetually dusty and drafty. In the fall, Mary develops a sore throat that lingers until spring. Sometimes she jolts awake in the middle of the night, coughing and gagging blood from her infected sore throat. Sometimes the throat infection becomes strep and she needs antibiotics.

My neighbor Marvin comes over and tells me I need to take responsibility for my wife's health and build her a house that's sealed from dust and easy to heat. He offers to lend me the money I need to build the house, interest free.

Mary and I love our little house in the woods. It's our cozy little cottage, where we now have three children and a woodshop. But we agree that Marvin is right.

I purchase some basic drafting tools, and pulling knowledge and skills from the drafting class I took in high school, Mary and I start drawing house plans. We don't know where to start. Every house we've lived in already had the rooms laid out. Now we're deciding where each room goes. We're figuring out where to place the stairway so it doesn't collide with some wall or room in the house. Somehow, as we pray, the plan comes together.

It's going to be a 36 x 32 house with a full basement, a steep 12/12 pitch roof, and a partial living space upstairs.

We construct it from used and salvaged building materials, rough lumber, and seconds from a local concrete block plant and a flooring factory. Somehow we patch it all together into a house far more suited to Mary's health and our growing family. Our church friends help with labor, and I'm deeply grateful. Now we have an insulated house, space to welcome more children into the family, and no more snow on our bed.

I set up my woodworking shop in our basement on the coarse gravel floor. Yes, it's crude, but at last I've got more working space and Mary doesn't have all the dust to put up with.

The locals admire our church people for craftsmanship and hard work at reasonable wages, so they hire us to build their houses. With different men pooling our abilities, we'll build an entire house from start to finish for a reasonable price.

We're building a house for Howard, our UPS driver, and I'm the logical choice for building the cabinets since I took a woodworking class in high school and have used those skills now for years. Usually the cabinetmaker sets up his table saw and other tools inside the house and builds the cabinets at the job site. But I want to build them in my basement.

After some coaxing, Howard agrees, and I'm eager to get started. These cabinets aren't going to be birdhouses or toy trucks. They'll occupy a prominent place in Howard's home for years to come, and I'm determined to build them to the highest standards.

I create a workspace in my basement. I set up a borrowed, rickety eight-inch table saw. To set the saw's fence, I need to measure in front of and behind the blade, making the space between the back of the blade just a tad wider than the front so the material doesn't bind and kick the piece I'm cutting back at me.

There's a support post in the middle of the basement. When I start cutting through a sheet of plywood, I only get halfway through before hitting the post. I have to turn off the saw and yell for Mary to come downstairs and help me rotate the entire saw so I can finish cutting through the plywood sheet.

One evening I back my old black International pickup to the opening in the basement and unload pine boards I've carefully chosen from the lumberyard. I set the table saw for two inches and rip several pieces for face frames. With a portable power saw, I measure, square, and cut several parts to the correct length. As I'm laying out parts on the simple, rough lumber workbench I've built, a huge wave of emotion washes over me. I feel alive. The darkness in me has retreated. I can barely function through my tears.

I want to do this for the rest of my life.

So many things I've tried have made my head spin and left me feeling confused and dissatisfied. By contrast, woodworking makes me serene and content. It fits me perfectly, as though I've been created for it.

Now I have a new problem: I don't know how to build cabinets to the quality I believe Howard expects from me. No one in our church knows much about building cabinets, so I search outside our faith community. I open the Yellow Pages and call every cabinet shop listed, asking them many questions.

One evening, while I'm sick with the flu, I call John Heubi, a woodworker who owns a shop 30 miles from me.

John also is down with the flu, and he enjoys discussing his craft. He's a master woodworker who was apprenticed by an old German cabinetmaker. John and I discuss woodworking into the wee hours for many nights. One night, John offers, "I'll teach you to become a woodworker."

Through many late-night conversations, John teaches me how to think like a craftsman. We never meet face-to-face until about a year and a half later. Had we met by chance, I wouldn't have recognized him. It doesn't seem logical that he can teach something so tangible—something you need to see and feel—so clearly by phone. And yet he does. No textbooks, no YouTube videos—simply words over a telephone.

For five years, John guides my heart and hands. Once we finally meet in person, he only spends a few hours in my shop.

I also find another mentor who teaches me to build beautiful, solid wood furniture. In the meantime, I read every woodworking book and magazine I can find, learning the finer points of the craft. When we visit people's homes, I peek inside their cabinets, trying to understand how they're constructed. I become a cabinet fanatic and am determined to learn how to make perfect cabinets.

For me, building beautiful cabinets is about more than tools, techniques, and grades of lumber. It's the art and romance of working with wood. John isn't a perfect man. He has family and business problems and sometimes is hot-tempered. But wood is his domain, and he's a master and true artist.

John built a dream shop with every tool and machine he could ever need for his craft. Then one terrible night, the shop burns down, and he loses everything. What is he going to do? How can he go on without his shop?

With his means of livelihood gone, John is forced into bankruptcy. Thinking he's got to start from the beginning, he sets up a table saw and router in his garage and does small woodworking projects for neighbors.

One night John tells me, "When I lost my shop and my tools, I thought I couldn't build cabinets anymore. Now I realize my skills aren't in my tools, but in my hands and my heart."

My mind lights up with a dawning realization. "A great craftsman doesn't build great things using the best tools and best materials," I say. "A great craftsman uses whatever he has and creates something beautiful from what is available. He has the *heart* of a craftsman."

That's a defining moment for both of us.

I think about how God takes broken lives and turns them into masterpieces. He is the ultimate craftsman, and we're created in his image, to be like him. No wonder I feel so alive and fulfilled when I'm turning rough wood into beautiful cabinets and furniture.

But even after years of learning from John and pushing myself to excel, I still believe I'm a failure. I can't imagine why customers buy from me. Even if my craftsmanship is a little better than some woodworkers, I don't understand why anyone comes to me.

Well, I think, *I guess I've got them all fooled. I must be a good liar. Other people make these things better and cheaper. How foolish must customers be to buy from me?*

Deep down I believe I'm lying when I tell people I'll deliver the best. A customer inquires about specialty cabinets and I say, "Sure, I can do that."

Then I panic because I don't know how to pull it off. Sometimes I can't get John on the phone. Then I get down on my face on the floor and cry out, "Jesus, you were a carpenter! You know how to do this, but I don't!"

God always comes through, and I somehow complete each project. I never understand, though, why God would help me—a liar and a broken person who only comes to him when I'm desperate.

Sometimes I finish a project and can't see anything but its flaws. I shake my head in disgust, call the customer, and let them know the project is finished.

"How did it turn out?" they ask eagerly.

"Not too good," I say with a sigh.

I hear disappointment on the other end. Then, when I deliver the cabinets, the customer inspects them and exclaims, "What were you talking about? This is far beyond my highest expectations!"

Mary and I invent a phrase for this. We call it Post-Finishing Blues. Even when I build good cabinets, I fixate on the flaws and believe I've failed. Learning to see my work through my customers' eyes will take many years. If I've done my best and they're pleased with the result, I'm not a failure, regardless of what my emotions tell me.

Chapter 22

DARKNESS IN THE CHURCH, LIGHT SHINING IN MY BUSINESS

As our children grow, they find ways to help in the cabinet shop, from sweeping floors to stacking lumber and eventually building cabinets. We work together in our garden, can food, and bake. While the church and many of the families are falling apart, we're finding a haven in our labors, both in the home and at work.

We have a new bishop. He's also the main teacher in our church-run school. His harsh, authoritarian ways hit us from every side. School spankings (frequently unjustified) take place nearly every day. It's not uncommon for him to accuse a child of misconduct. If the child denies it, the bishop spanks him twice: first for misconduct and then for lying. So sometimes our children "lie" and admit to something they didn't do just to avoid two spankings. We appeal to the bishop about how he treats our children, but daring to question his authority is considered rebellion.

I don't realize until years later how much the church leaders have been manipulating people against each other. The leaders exploit any differences they can, especially between those born into the church and those who join from the outside—like our family. Mistrust grows until we all hold one another at arm's length, afraid to be honest or authentic about anything.

Trying to cope with our unsafe church environment, I seek relief in food and my work. My weight balloons out of control. When I stuff myself, I feel better momentarily, then drown in shame afterward.

While Mary is pregnant with our middle son, Josh, an ultrasound reveals a placenta previa, where the placenta blocks the birth canal. We have little money and no insurance, and the nearest hospital equipped to help us is 90 miles away in Chattanooga. Because of the risks, Mary is told to lie flat on her back—completely still—near the hospital until the birth. So we get a room in a hotel attached to the hospital.

For seven long weeks Mary lies flat on her back in that lonely room, listening to the air conditioner and counting dots in the ceiling tiles. Since the church doesn't allow us to use television, radio, or tape players, she has nothing to help pass the time.

Meanwhile, an administrator from a hospital in a nearby town, Sewanee, Tennessee, brings me a sketch of some cabinets he wants me to build. He seems demanding about exactly what he wants, when he wants it, and how much he's willing to pay.

His pushiness annoys me, and I want to turn him away, but we desperately need money. With no insurance, Mary in a hotel, and the upcoming hospital stay upon us, our bills are piling up. I swallow my annoyance and build his cabinets. The administrator must be pleased with me because he brings me more jobs. I'm willing to tolerate his abrasive personality because we need work.

It turns out the Sewanee hospital is owned by the hospital in Chattanooga, and their corporate offices are in the same hotel building where Mary is staying. I bring pictures of my cabinets to the corporate office, show them to the division's vice president, and tell him,

"I love making cabinets and would be happy to build anything you need."

He studies the pictures and says, "We'll have a lot of work in your area in about six months. Give me a fair price, and I'll send you lots of work."

Give me a fair price, and I'll send you lots of work. I've heard that before. That sounds like a familiar brush-off. A customer pressures me to do a job for a low price and promises me more work. But once they get their discounted cabinets, I never hear from them again.

Meanwhile, the hospital in Sewanee has replaced their administrator with a more congenial man. One day he invites me into their basement.

"We're cleaning everything out," he says. "Look around and take anything you want."

Among my finds are a gurney, a cart, and best of all, a huge 1,000-watt operating room light on a portable stand. I construct a plywood platform on our basement's gravel floor and build every cabinet on that platform. With the 1,000-watt light aimed at the cabinets, I can see everything in fine detail.

I tell myself: *I want these cabinets so flawless that if Solomon was searching for someone to do the woodwork in his temple, God would point to me and say, "Here's your man. He has my heart, and the heart of a craftsman."*

After seven and a half long weeks of waiting in that Chattanooga hotel room, our son Josh is born by Cesarean section. We almost lose him at birth, and he spends time in the neo-natal intensive care unit (NICU) before we can bring him home. Our hospital bills have soared, and although our church generously helps pay some of them, we have accumulated considerable debt. It's going to take me a couple of years to pay it down.

* * * * *

Just like he promised, right around six months after the hospital's vice president said he'd send me more cabinet work, I get a call from a nearby hospital. He had passed my number to Lew Mashburn, administrator at Coffee Medical Center, in Manchester, Tennessee. Lew's secretary Doris calls and invites me to his office to discuss what he wants.

When I arrive, Doris smiles and says, "Mr. Mashburn is expecting you." After escorting me into his office, she serves us tea and cakes on a silver platter.

"I hear you do good millwork," Lew says as he shakes my hand firmly.

"Yes, I do," I say, believing I'm lying. I still don't believe I do good work, but I'm desperate for the opportunity.

Lew shows me a wardrobe plan. "I need one of these right away," he says. "How much will it cost?"

"I charge ten dollars per hour, plus materials." I'm stretching the truth, because six dollars per hour is my current hourly rate.

"Okay," Lew says without flinching. Then he rolls out some other plans. "I want you to start on all this when you finish the first part," he says.

After perusing through the plans, I gasp, "That's a whole year of work!"

"That's right," he agrees, like it's no big deal.

I leave the hospital floating in the clouds. Then it hits me: I don't know how to build hospital cabinets.

I panic all the way home. When I get home, I call John Heubi, and he explains how to build plastic laminated hospital cabinets. Still doubting myself, I call Lew and tell him I don't know how to build hospital cabinets. Instead of canceling the work as I expect, Lew invites me to Chattanooga for a day. He lends me a camera, and together we tour hospitals, snapping photos of every style of cabinet they use.

For the next several months, I work feverishly, trying to please Lew. Every time the phone rings, I'm sure Lew is calling to say, "Phil, I realize now you can't do this job. Sorry, I'm getting someone else."

But that dreaded call never comes. Instead, he calls again and again to tell me about the next projects he has for me.

I spend many years waiting for that termination call—not only from Lew, but from other clients as well. The call never comes.

Many years later, I reconnect with Lew and ask, "Did you realize I was lying to you when I said I knew what I was doing?"

He laughs and says, "Oh, I knew that. Your self-doubt was obvious. The thing is, I believed in you."

At least one of us did.

I think about John Heubi, who told me in one of our late night calls it's not in the tools but in the hands and heart. Maybe God is giving me a craftsman's heart. Maybe I can succeed at something.

> Maybe God is giving me a craftsman's heart. Maybe I can succeed at something.

One day an architect calls me in a panic. A contractor, Bencor, has a project running late, and the cabinet shop they contracted with has backed out on them. It's a complex reception desk for the Boy Scout headquarters in Chattanooga. They need it right away, and I need work!

When I visit the jobsite, I discover I'm supposed to build to an architect's set of plans, and I can't read the plans. I've always created my own drawings from concepts the customers give me. The architect and contractor keep explaining it to me, but I don't get it.

Finally, they say, "Go home and study it. It'll make sense."

I head home and submit a bid of a little more than four thousand dollars. They accept, send me a contract, and I start working. Still, I can't figure out how to build it. The plans make no sense to me.

Panicked, I spiral out of control. The project manager who hired me no longer works at Bencor, so I can't contact him.

It's a large, complex combination reception desk and display case, with compound angles, Formica cabinet faces, oak frames, glass displays and tops, and metal drawers.

Realizing this project is over my head, I tell myself, "I'll call and tell them I can't keep my commitment, and they'll have to sue me."

But I call John first.

John senses my frenzy.

"Phil," he says in a calm voice, "you should be able to do this project standing on your head."

"But I don't . . . I have no idea how—"

John offers to come out and help me. While I'm waiting for John, I get down on my face and desperately pray, "Jesus, you were a carpenter. You know how to do this; I don't. Please show me."

This is one of the few times John comes to my place. Standing alongside me, looking at the plans with me, he tells me, "Calm down. Slow down. Take a step at a time. Let's start with the first thing you understand . . ."

I slow down and find my pace.

To my surprise, the project comes together and I complete it three days early. After I install it, I step back and inspect my work, and for once I honestly can say, "This is excellent." I can't deny the beautiful piece of craftsmanship in front of me. I can't put myself down, no matter how insecure I feel.

The construction company, Bencor, is owned by Bob Corker, who later becomes a U.S. Senator from Tennessee (leaving that seat in 2019). Next Bencor offers me a project doing some complex, curved-exterior millwork. We build and deliver a $24,000 project to an apartment complex in Florida, and everything clicks on that job.

Bencor is satisfied, so I ask if they have any other work.

"We're building stores for Walmart. Would you like to look at a project?"

Would I! Thus, a wild new adventure begins. Eventually, we complete more than 850 cabinet projects for Walmart, including their first three stores in Alaska and the first store in Hawaii.

* * * * *

In 1984, soon before my first excommunication from the church, I build my first real cabinet shop outside our home. We disassemble an old mechanic shop, haul the cement blocks, steel trusses, entrance doors, and a large overhead door up the mountain to our property. I spend days cleaning used cement blocks until my hands are bleeding and calloused.

It's a huge project, but opportunities for good work at nice profits keep coming my way. Through a few financial miracles, I've paid off the debt from Josh's birth and I complete the shop building debt free!

Now sometimes I silently stand alone in the shop, lift my eyes to Heaven, and weep tears of gratitude. Other times, when I'm overwhelmed or in a bind with a project, I fall on my face and cry out to God: "You know how to do this! I don't. Please help me!"

God knows I don't want wealth, yet wealth is coming my way. By 1990, we're shipping projects all over the United States.

> My hands produce good work. Customers are pleased. So why is my brain on fire? What's this fiery ball of rage in my gut?

My hands produce good work. Customers are pleased. So why is my brain on fire? What's this fiery ball of rage in my gut? I read the Bible, faithfully attend church, and follow the church's rules. I often ask myself, "Why do they call this 'Gospel' the good news?"

I'm afraid to ask the church people because I think they know something I don't, and they'll shame or shun me for being an imposter who doesn't know the secret. And yet, the more the church criticizes me, the more God blesses my work and business. Why doesn't someone give God the memo that I'm a loser? I'm experiencing such pleasure working with my wife and children on Walmart facilities across the nation—even while the church is excommunicating me, doing all they can, it seems, to deepen my depression. It also seems that the more God honors my woodwork, the greater I feel church's disapproval.

Only the therapy of woodworking and the love I experience from my young family keeps hope alive in my heart.

Chapter 23

A Song For God

Ever since that turbulent night in 1969 when I was wasted on drugs and wanted to take my life, I never lost my desire to connect with music. That night, when Wally played the guitar and sitar, music penetrated every fiber of me, providing a wonderful release. That night my crude attempt to write my thoughts and feelings was the beginning of a lifelong friendship with music and writing. To this day, writing and music are still among my closest friends. I love the way words and music come together drawing me closer to my spirit and to Heaven. Whenever I struggle with the ugly dramas around me, I retreat into my safe, sacred sanctuary of writing and music.

One quiet evening, I'm standing alone in my shop and think, *What if God allows me to write one hymn?*

This idea grabs me, and I often pray, "God, what an honor it would be if I could write a hymn for you. Let me write at least one hymn before I die."

One morning I'm sitting at the kitchen table looking through a hymnbook. I can't read music, so I make up a tune and start singing the words.

Oh, when the tears are flowing from sorrow's faded eyes.
When lonely hearts are aching, beneath the cloudy skies.

As I'm singing to Mary, the song floods me with joy. I jump up from the table and hop around like an excited little boy, exclaiming, "I did it! I did it!"

I hurry to the home of our young minister, a man with a soft heart for music, and eagerly begin singing.

"Hold on a second!" he says, grabbing a pencil and paper.

He writes the notes as I'm singing! After that, the minister and his wife often join Mary and me around our table, singing my song, as we try to compose four-part harmonies into it.

Something inside me is waking up. Although I'm imprisoned in a dark religious system, no one can stop me from singing and writing, and that feels amazing and powerful. Now I'm hungry to write more hymns, so I search bookstores for the stories behind the old hymns. I fall in love with the poetry of John Newton and Frances Havergal and compose my own music to their poems. I'd print the famous author's name on the left and my name—the composer—on the right, smiling and thinking, *I never thought I'd see my name next to John Newton or Frances Havergal!*

When my mother comes to visit, I want to give her a special treat and sing my new song for her. We invite about twenty church people into our living room for a casual concert. Unfortunately, when we sing my song, my hymn falls apart. The harmonies that worked so well with four of us sitting around a table become a train wreck in a larger group.

Frustrated, I visit the local library and search the Nashville and Chattanooga phone books for someone who can teach me to write harmonies. My search turns up nothing until one Sunday some dinner guests tell me about Gerald Moore, the head of the music department at Lipscomb University in Nashville. They say he's especially skilled in writing four-part vocal harmonies.

I call Gerald, and he agrees to mentor me for an hourly fee. Gerald and I mesh from the beginning. He teaches me the fundamentals of harmony, how to create chords and chord progressions, and how to progress logically through a song. I compose melodies to some of Havergal's and Newton's poems, and unlike my first attempt, these melodies work in a larger group!

* * * * *

A few months later, our family travels to Costa Rica to visit churches planted by our denomination. We sing our songs to the local people, and they enjoy our singing but don't understand the English lyrics. That bothers me.

I tell one of the missionaries, "If I write hymns in English, I might become famous eventually, but I won't make much eternal difference since we already have so many hymns in English. But if I write hymns in Spanish, I'll be preparing feasts for people who can't repay me."

My friend agrees and tells me about a Mennonite publisher in New Mexico who is creating a new Spanish hymnal. "You might want to contact them," he suggests.

After returning home, I call the publishing company, and they confirm they're compiling a Spanish hymnal. I volunteer to help, and they send me several songs to work on. Using the Spanish I learned earlier in Mexico and the music theory Gerald Moore taught me, I go to work.

Our family spends many hours singing together and developing the music. Sometimes we invite church friends over to help. Some songs are easy and come together without much effort, while others require hours of painstaking work. I bring each song into my sessions with Gerald, and he helps me create the best chords and harmonies.

After working on the project for a few months, we pack up our old fifteen-passenger van and drive from Tennessee to New Mexico to meet the people compiling the Spanish hymnbook. When we arrive at the address they gave us, the men standing on the porch have no beards or suspenders, and they're wearing short-sleeved shirts. Mary gets out and asks if we've come to the right house.

"You've found us," one says as they smile and introduce themselves.

Why don't they look the same as us? This is our first experience with Mennonites who don't dress like us. Because we don't want to become defiled by them, we seriously consider turning around and driving home. But since we've driven 1,500 miles, we agree to take a risk and stay.

We work with a small team at the publishing house, combing through hundreds of songs, choosing a few at a time, singing together, and composing melodies or adding harmonies. We sing for eight hours, then quit for the day. Spanish is such a lovely, singable language, and many times I'll stop to cry at the beauty of the songs. But I also argue with these people about how liberal their lifestyle is. The men are supposed to have beards. The women need larger head coverings. Driving cars that aren't black and using tape players is wrong. Can't they understand how angry God is at their worldliness?

These people don't keep the rules we're convinced Christians are supposed to keep, but they also appear much freer and happier than we are. When I talked to them on the phone before we came, they always struck me as sincere, godly, and loving.

Now that we're with them, we perceive they accept people like us who are different from them—even if we don't accept them. Our church flatly refuses to accept this church because of a few external differences. So how is it that we sense so much godliness in people we believe can't be Christians? They're more like Jesus than some of those in my own church!

I'm conflicted. In theory, I know God sees the heart, but our church's concepts have been so drilled into me that I can't conceive of Christianity that isn't all about external appearance. However, Mary and I are discovering the possibility that God's heart could be bigger than we think it is.

* * * * *

After returning home, we continue working on Spanish hymns for several more months. Mary and I plan another trip to New Mexico to continue collaborating on the project, but then one of our church leaders visits me.

"I talked to the minister in New Mexico, and he said they don't need your help after all," he tells me.

Devastated, I call the New Mexico pastor and ask what caused this change of heart.

Surprised, he says, "I didn't tell your pastor we don't need your help. In fact, I said how much we appreciate your help, and I appealed to him to allow you to work with us despite our church differences."

I'm scared of our leaders, but I have to confront this discrepancy. When I do, the church leader refuses to make eye contact with me and sits frozen for a long time without saying a word. At last, he says, "We don't want you going so far away and leaving your children behind."

So I spend thousands of dollars on plane tickets so our younger children can fly to New Mexico with us. Those still in school stay at the homes of various people in the church. Although we proceed with the trip plans, I'm disturbed by what happened. This is only one of many occasions when our leaders are less than honest. Furthermore, we sense them using mind control and emotional manipulation, twisting Scriptures to make us feel guilt and shame for things we haven't done. But we don't know how to prove it.

Singing Spanish hymns to God is my escape from their control since our leaders don't understand Spanish. I sing with freedom, not worrying whether they'll find fault with the songs and accuse me

I sing with freedom, not worrying whether they'll find fault with the songs and accuse me of some vague sin. This freedom is a gift of sheer grace from God because our church continues to implode.

of some vague sin. This freedom is a gift of sheer grace from God because our church continues to implode. Members are constantly in conflict with each other. The bickering is often driven by absurd issues like the style of hats the men wear or what hubcaps we should allow on our cars.

Carol, a blind lady, comes to our community and stays in our house for around six weeks. She is interested in our beliefs and eager to learn our way of life.

I am deeply troubled as I realize that because of her blindness, Carol can't see all the things that define our Christianity: our plain clothes, our simple houses, our black cars. How can we communicate what we believe is important when she can't see any of it?

Furthermore, I'm painfully aware that although she can't see our outward attempts at perfection, Carol hears our ugly tone of voice as we speak harshly to our children and Mary and I bicker.

I think about the man in Richmond who told me to find something that worked for at least ten years before presenting it to others. I thought I had found it, but can I pretend our church's system works when our perfect exteriors hide internal chaos?

No one seems happy, least of all me. I somehow believe I'm the main cause of all the church's problems. I slide deeper into confusion and spend sleepless nights haunted by nightmares from my past. My sleep is often interrupted by tremors so violent they wake both Mary and me. I'm getting only three or four hours of shallow sleep each night and swallowing more than seventy pills a day. Prescriptions, herbs, and supplements don't help. I turn to food for comfort and gain massive weight.

Around that time, my body begins to fail. If I walk for more than a half hour, I hurt from head to toe for days. Although I don't know it, I need a hip replacement.

I'm 43 years old, anxious, depressed, exhausted, and crippled.

Mary fears I will soon die.

* * * * *

A doctor I visit in Nashville recommends chelation therapy, so for several weeks I drive 90 miles to Nashville three times a week and sit with a drip in my arm for three-hour sessions.

I use that time to deep-dive into the Bible. A concordance by my side, I research the events surrounding David's psalms and take many notes. Then I study Jacob's final blessings to his sons and where those blessings went many generations later.

The treatments are spaced so I can spend one night a week in Nashville.

A guy in Nashville named Steve has expressed interest in our church, so I ask if I can spend a night at his place.

"Sure, come on over," he says.

I arrive at Steve's place around 7:30 that evening. We talk for several hours, and I head for bed. As I'm drifting off to sleep, I hear Steve yelling and cursing from another room in the house.

"No! No! I'm not going to do it!" he's yelling. "Leave me alone!" I don't know if Steve is fighting with someone, but I'm so exhausted I fall asleep.

Around 3 in the morning I jolt awake and can't get back to sleep. I go outside and sit on the steps of Steve's small porch. The Nashville night is still except for the sleepy *clackity clack* of a distant train. A soft, misty halo surrounds the streetlamps, reflecting a black shine from the rain-soaked streets.

I feel more torn up inside than ever. But because I'm supposed to act like a Christian, I must always pretend everything is okay. As I think about my wife and each of my nine children, I'm engulfed in the deepest gut-wrenching agony I've ever experienced.

Years earlier, at Planet Earth, I had cried for my pain. Now I'm crying not only for my pain but for the pain I've been causing my wife and our children as well, and for the future pain they could suffer because I don't know how to be a godly husband and father or make wise decisions. My pain is ten times—no, one hundred, or even a thousand—times greater than anything I've ever experienced.

> As I think about my wife and each of my nine children, I'm engulfed in the deepest gut-wrenching agony I've ever experienced.

"Oh God," I pray, "please don't ever let me make a decision that would hurt my wife or any of my children. Before I do that, kill me and throw me into hell."

Now I'm engulfed in the worst convulsive sobs I've ever experienced. I'm crying so hard my body has nothing left, but my soul is still weeping.

Exhausted, I return to bed and fall into a fitful sleep.

In the morning, Steve asks, "Did you hear me yelling last night? I'm sorry about that. Yesterday I took my college finals. I found out I failed and won't be graduating." He pauses; I sense he wants to share more. "I was so devastated I bought some cocaine and got high. Last night Satan kept telling me to murder you, and I was arguing with him."

Chapter 24

A NEW BEGINNING

After twenty years of trying hard to be a good Christian and give my children the father I never had, I'm beyond exhausted. The church has repeatedly shunned me and placed me on "proving" for not measuring up. I work in the shop on most days from 3 am to midnight. Although it's rewarding to ship cabinets all over the country and make more money than we need, I'm too lost in the wars inside my head to enjoy any of it.

My consuming physical pain continues. I've been to several doctors, but none of them diagnoses my problem. I guilt and shame myself because I think I'm too lazy. One day I'm looking in the mirror and notice muscles on my right hip. But my left hip appears hollow. Mary pokes on both sides and says she feels muscles on the right hip but on the left hip she feels skin and bone. I book an appointment with an orthopedic surgeon. He takes a few X-rays and shows me I need a total hip replacement.

I ask the church leaders to anoint me with oil for healing like the Bible says in James 5:14-15. Predictably, they can't give me an easy yes. The long process includes an investigation, church approval, and, if I clear all the hurdles, a solemn event that lasts an entire evening. Because the ministers hear that we plan to visit a church in another state, they refuse to anoint me, correctly suspecting that we're thinking about moving.

I drive over to the sawmill owned by our bishop, hoping to appeal this decision. He and his deacon stand in the muddy lot, and my heart becomes awkwardly silent as I look at the hard, stern faces of my spiritual leaders.

A voice whispers inside me: *Now if any man have not the Spirit of Christ, he is none of his* (Romans 8:9, KJV). After twenty years with these people, I'm realizing the truth for the first time: I don't see or feel the Spirit of Christ in these men's spirits or their lives. Their heavy-handed rule over the church is marked by manipulation, shame, guilt, and complicated rules.

I think, *If I tell them, they'll immediately label me a heretic and excommunicate me again,* so I remain silent. Yet, as though awakening from a dream, I'm admitting to myself that the men I've been following for the past two decades haven't been leading me closer to Christ.

A day or two later, Mary appeals to the leaders on my behalf, but they're still adamantly against anointing me. Then they learn that we've postponed moving to another church, so they tell me they're willing to come to our house and conduct the anointing service.

* * * * *

A few evenings later, the ministers and my family are assembled in our living room. We sing a few hymns and read from James 5 about confessing our faults to each other and anointing the sick person for healing.

One by one, each person in the room confesses their faults. When the bishop's turn comes, he says, "I'm not aware of any faults in my life."

Stunned, I respectfully ask the ministers to join me in the next room. I close the door, turn trembling to the bishop, and say, "We all have faults, including you. Unless you're willing to confess them like the rest of us, I don't have faith to proceed with the anointing."

As is his habit whenever he's put on the spot, he stares silently and coldly at me for a long time. When we return to the living room where the family is waiting, he says, "Brother Phillip won't be proceeding with the anointing tonight."

After an awkward pause, the ministers leave.

Soon, the bishop is calling me early practically every morning, asking to meet with me so he can "bring another concern." I start removing my phone from the hook so I can get dressed and eat breakfast in peace. When he finally comes over, his "concerns" usually make no sense to me, but they leave me feeling condemned, confused, and victimized.

One day I'm walking from the shop to the house carrying a three-foot steel pipe that we use for woodworking clamps. As I repeatedly swing it like a baseball bat, I fantasize bashing the leader's skull with my pipe. Horrified by my murderous thoughts, I realize it's time to leave this dark place.

Around this time, a friend from Kentucky invites us to visit their church for a weekend, and we enjoy our visit. We sense God's presence there, and Mary and I feel peace about moving to that community. Although it's also a very conservative group, people in our church warn us that the folks in Kentucky are too liberal. Some of their homes have luxuries such as carpets and dishwashers! Joining them supposedly means we're drifting into "the world."

Despite the warnings, I know I'm not moving to Kentucky to become more worldly. I'm trying to find the God I thought I had met two decades earlier.

* * * * *

We purchase 25 acres with a house and barn and a fantastic view of the rolling Kentucky countryside. The house is like a Swiss chalet, with a large fireplace, spiral staircase, and a steep roof with split cedar shingles.

On moving day, Arlin, a man who's been excommunicated from our Tennessee church, comes to help us load our trucks. The bishop keeps bugging me to tell Arlin to leave. I try to ignore the bishop. As we're driving away, the bishop approaches me once more to say, "Phillip, you must tell Arlin to leave."

I look at him and say, "You're the bishop here. That's your problem." A strange sadness overwhelms me as we drive away. It feels strange because I don't regret leaving the church that defined my world for two decades. Instead, I'm sad because I'm leaving my neighbors, the simple country folk who loved and accepted me even while I judged them as sinners for not dressing and believing the same as us.

* * * * *

Our family quickly settles into the routine of our new life in Kentucky. We build a new shop, and our woodworking business continues to thrive.

I'm enjoying simple pleasures such as light fixtures instead of bare bulbs. Our new bishop is a jolly, rotund man who loves to laugh. Although he takes his church responsibilities seriously, he's not against having fun, as our previous leaders had been. And he doesn't try to regulate every detail of our lives.

In fact, one day he tells me to stop bugging him about every decision I make. For example, when I think a riding mower could make it easier to maintain our large property, I ask his permission—as I formerly was conditioned to do.

"Stop it, Phillip!" he says after several such incidents. "You don't have to ask my permission for these things. If the church doesn't have a rule about something, you're free to make the decision you think best for your family."

I'm bewildered and insecure with this freedom. Without authoritarian leaders directing my every decision, how will I avoid breaking

I'm bewildered and insecure with this freedom. Without authoritarian leaders directing my every decision, how will I avoid breaking an unwritten rule and getting into trouble?

an unwritten rule and getting into trouble?

Despite my insecurity, Mary and the children are happier and freer than was possible in our old church. This community began as a horse and buggy Amish church but recently joined the conservative Mennonites. Now they're driving cars, which causes consternation in the community. (As one woman from church told us, "When I'm driving and see a car coming toward me, I instinctively head for the ditch.")

Because of their Amish background, most families speak Pennsylvania Dutch. Along with their language, some of their cultural practices appear strange to us, but they welcome us warmly, and we feel loved and accepted.

* * * * *

After our move, I continue working on the Spanish hymnal until its publication in 1996. *Himnos de la Iglesia* (Hymns of the Church) is a beautiful hardcover book containing five hundred hymns that will be enjoyed by many churches in Latin America for many years.

I'm also free to explore my love for writing and get several articles published in our denomination's periodicals. Hoping to improve my writing skills, I attend a writers' conference in Virginia. One of the classes is called Writing from Perspective.

"Writing from a single perspective is more powerful than trying to write everything about a scene," the teacher explains. "For example, if you draw a house from one point of view, it makes more sense than trying to draw the house from every side. The person looking at the picture mentally fills in details they can't see."

The teacher recommends a book, *Write to Discover Yourself,* by Ruth Vaughn.

"To learn to write from perspective," Vaughn writes, "start with yourself. Write from your own perspective. Write about your childhood, how you saw life from your child's eyes. Recall childhood scenes and relive them. Describe the sound of your father's voice. How did he smell? How did he act in different situations? How did that make you feel?"[3]

When I begin that exercise, my emotional dam breaks. Within a month I've written around ten thousand words. I organize it into an essay called "Weeping May Endure for a Night, But Joy Comes in the Morning."

I share the essay with my mom and a few church leaders, asking them not to share it with anyone else. Despite my request, they pass the manuscript around, and people urge me to publish it.

Encouraged by my ministers and my mom, I publish my story in book form, call it *Weeping May Endure for a Night,* and to my surprise, it sells thousands of copies. The resulting attention and notoriety go to my head, and I believe my identity and worth is tied to public recognition. People who read my story form favorable impressions of me, and I bask in their approval. But because I simultaneously run roughshod over the people closest to me, they distance themselves from me.

Everyone likes me—except the people who know me in real life.

Although we outwardly appear a peaceful, well-adjusted Christian family, I'm still moody and unpredictable. Emotional eating has elevated my weight to new highs, and I'm prone to violent fits of rage.

One day one of our sons unintentionally hurts one of his siblings.

I fly into a rage, grabbing my son and slamming him against the wall. I shout as I ball my fist, rear back, and act like I'm going to punch him in the mouth.

"It was an accident," my 10-year-old son pleads.

"I don't care. Bend over the bed!" I scream. My son is trembling all over as I blister his rear with a wooden dowel rod. In pain, he crumbles to the floor, wailing.

"Get up!" I yell.

"I can't!" he sobs.

"Do what I tell you!"

I swing the dowel rod wildly over his back and legs. After several wallops, he stands up and bends over the bed, his entire body trembling as he receives my final blows to his legs and behind.

Suddenly, flashbacks of my childhood arrest me. I see myself turning into my father, and this time my son is the broken, weeping little boy cowering by the bed.

Filled with self-loathing and remorse, I barely contain the inner scream of pain that sweeps over me.

"Go to your room," I command my son. When he leaves, I close the door and drop my massively bulky body onto the bed. My children's faces flash through my mind. I see my oldest son, Noah, when he was only two years old, and me spanking him practically every day, his cries echoing in the caverns of my mind.

"You need to spank the evil out of children!" our church leaders in Tennessee had lectured us repeatedly from the pulpit. "Foolishness is bound up in their hearts. If horses and goats can be trained, so can children! We must break their evil will. We must use the rod to beat it out of them."

Children are regarded not as innocent, but as little sinners, born evil, who can't do anything right.

I'm convinced I have biblical reasons for beating my children physically and emotionally. It's what we're taught—our way of life. Other church families do it. During the church service children get pinched or taken outside for whippings for not sitting still or not paying attention.

Never a day passes without my children receiving one or more spankings. Mary's family members often complain that we're too harsh, but I dismiss their concerns because I reason they're not qualified to give *me* advice.

When I'm honest with myself, I have to admit I have turned into my father. I'm helplessly trapped inside the spirit of his rages—and powerless to change myself.

But God, I'm a Christian! That's supposed to make a difference! Why am I doing these things?

I drop heavily onto our bed and rock back and forth in agony of soul. I don't want to become my dad, but it's happening! I'm becoming the monster my dad said I am!

I look at my life.

Who am I?

I'm a church member who faithfully attends services. I read the Bible. I pray. I tithe. I'm a successful businessman. My cabinet shop is doing well financially.

I'm a husband. I have the best wife anyone could want.

I'm a father. I have nine great children who are hardworking, well-adjusted, and beautiful.

I have a church that's a great blessing to me. We have more freedom here than in our previous community, and while their Pennsylvania Dutch ways are still strange to us, we all thrive in the healthier environment.

All of this should add up to one happy man. Phillip Cohen *should* be happy.

Instead, my old demons have followed me into this new place. My new beginning is an illusion. I haven't changed, and I have no answers.

Chapter 25

NIGHT SESSIONS

Although our new life is going better in many ways, I still don't have any close relationships. Whenever I get close to people, I find constant fault with them. There's always *something* about *someone* that bothers me. Fueled by my fear of rejection, I spend hours journaling everything I think is wrong with other people. Like the bishop in our previous church who constantly confronted me with "concerns," I hit people with all my criticisms about their real and imaginary flaws. Understandably, people avoid me.

Since my book has been published, I think they'll finally understand me once they read it and feel the pain I've suffered, but it doesn't work. In fact, in some ways, it seems to have backfired—more people are pulling away from me.

I tell myself that since I read the Bible regularly and support the church's rules, those people are wrong and I'm right. Everyone's out to get me, especially the leaders. They're persecuting me, and I'm a martyr.

Mary's struggling because she genuinely loves these people and feels loved in return. Her gifts are teaching, organizing, and serving, and her gifts are recognized, appreciated, and utilized by the church; she's leading sewing and hospitality committees and teaching Sunday school.

Our children also love the church and enjoy organized youth activities that were forbidden in our previous community. The older ones are church members, and they're accepted and well liked. I'm the only person in our family who doesn't fit in.

When I'm alone, especially at night, I know I'm the problem, but I don't know what to do about it. Several times I think about taking my life and removing my obnoxious, rotten personality and miserable, obese carcass from this world. I feel certain everyone would be better off without me. Oh sure, they would grieve, and people would say, "Poor Phillip," but they'd soon get over it.

However, I'm afraid to kill myself because suicide is murder, and murderers go to hell. If I'm living in hell now, killing myself would lock me into eternal hell. I believe God has brought me into a world I didn't ask for and demands I either get with the program or go to hell. I ask God to kill me so I can go to Heaven. I even hope my overeating drives me to an early grave. Many nights I lie in bed, facing the wall, praying for my heart to stop.

Sometimes I spend all day in bed, paralyzed by depression. My passions and dark fantasies attack me with horrific force. I'm moody and angry with everyone. Day and night I hear screams in my head: my dad screaming at Mom, my siblings, and me; my mom screaming for help that never comes; and me stifling the screams in my huge inner void that only I can hear.

Like living nightmares—only it's in the middle of the day—I hear the sickening thud of Dad slamming Mom's head into the wall. I feel the sting and thud of both ends of Dad's belt hitting me all over my face and body.

"No, Dad! No, *please!*" the little boy in me pleads at his relentless blows as I'm raising my hands to protect my body and face, only to feel his vicious belt stinging my arms.

> In my brief moments of sanity, they include me in their conversations and plans. When I withdraw and become morose and sullen, they respectfully give me space. But none of them understand.

LSD flashbacks explode in my brain—and they're no fun the second time around.

I'm going crazy, and I know it.

Through it all, Mary and our children surround me with love and grace. My older children accept my mood swings since it's all they've ever known. In my brief moments of sanity, they include me in their conversations and plans. When I withdraw and become morose and sullen, they respectfully give me space. But none of them understand what's happening inside me.

Mary finds strength to continue as a sweet wife and mother despite my lack of participation. Sometimes she breaks down under the strain. But most of the time she's pleasant and kind and overlooks my craziness with supernatural grace and love. Because of our church's beliefs about women, Mary has no one to unload her heart to. The women relate to one another socially, which is more than we had in our previous church. But they don't communicate on spiritual and emotional levels. The only way Mary makes it through another day is to believe someday I'll be healed and become normal.

She later tells me she didn't know a human could drop as low as I did and survive.

I'm losing hope that I'll ever be healed. If Christianity and the church can't help me, I believe I'll always have to live with my crippled mind and emotions. I'm beyond desperate.

I tell Mary, "I want to check myself into a mental hospital."

"Phillip," she says, "you don't need to go away to a hospital. We don't have much work right now for the shop, we don't have any debt, and we live a mile off the road. No one will bother us back here. Stay here and let your dam break in this peaceful place."

I'm willing to try her suggestion, at least for a few weeks. Inwardly, I let my dam break.

Around that time, our septic tank gets full, and sewage backs up into the toilets and bathtubs. The entire house smells and feels brown. I call a septic service I find in the phone book, and the man shows up within an hour.

The house stinks and some of us are "holding our stuff in" because we have to avoid using the plumbing.

It takes the guy most of the day to clean out our septic system.

"I've never seen such a clogged-up mess," he says as he hands me the bill. "The tank was packed so full I had to use a garden hose and a digging iron to get it all loose. It took three truckloads to get the tank empty." He shakes his head at the memory.

That night I wake up and hear the man's voice in my head: "It took three truckloads to get the tank empty."

That's what you're like inside, another voice whispers in my head. *You're packed full and overflowing with pain and sin from your past.*

Passing before my mind's eye, I see the festering wounds, the ruined relationships, the uncontrollable fantasies and appetites. I think, *My life stinks inside and out. I'm packed tight full of human waste!*

I'm spiraling out of control, sucking downward into eternal darkness. A huge, fiery ball of rage in my gut holds back suppressed screams. It's locking my jaw as I'm gritting my teeth to subconsciously hold back the screams. When I sleep, my teeth grind and grind until they're worn down shorter.

Dad's words echo in deafening roars in my head: "I've created a monster! You'll never amount to anything!"

Night after night, I'm terrified. On nights when I can't take any more, I shake Mary to wake her. She turns on the bedside lamp, which creates a small pool of light and a glow of hope in the pitch blackness of my soul.

"I need you to . . . to do something," I beg.

"Do you want to pray?"

"I can't. Could you read the Bible to me?"

Mary reaches for her Bible and reads aloud from Psalms. "In you, O Lord, do I take refuge. Let me never be put to shame: in your righteousness deliver me!"

Her sweet, steady voice pours into me like warm, soothing oil. "Incline your ear to me; rescue me speedily! Be a rock of refuge for me and a strong fortress to save me."

Our midnight episodes become routine. We call them Night Sessions.

"Can you get a writing tablet?" I ask one night.

Mary stops reading and picks up a tablet and pen. "What's going on inside?" she asks, writing my responses.

"There's a huge ball of pain and rage right here below my rib cage."

As Mary writes, I tell her about the time I thought Dad was going to chop my fingers off with a meat cleaver as punishment for lying.

"Are you angry at someone?" Mary asks.

"I'm always angry at someone."

Mary writes as I tell her everyone I hate, including God and myself.

"I feel more secure when I'm in conflict, especially with people in authority," I tell her, revealing my raw insides. "I remember one time back in Tennessee thinking it had been a few months since I was in trouble with the ministers. I didn't like that because I thought they had given up on me. I intentionally create conflicting relationships because that feels like love to me."

Night after night, we share these dialogues and Mary writes down our conversations. For more than twenty years I've tried putting on a godly front while hiding the truth about me. I'm surrounded by church people who teach and practice the same thing: stuff your real emotional self deep down inside yourself and wear your Christianity on the outside.

I don't know how they're so successful doing that it; it's not working for me. What's happening inside me is too powerful to contain behind my pious outward appearance.

A fellow writer named Dallas has been mentoring me with my writing, helping me hone my skills and encouraging me to publish. After I complete *Weeping May Endure for a Night,* I tell Dallas I'd like to find another writing project. After tossing around a few ideas, Dallas sends me several Prayer Support letters from Pablo Yoder, an American Mennonite missionary living deep in the jungles of Nicaragua.

The letters tell of robberies, rapes, kidnappings, and murders in this recently war-torn nation.

Intrigued, I write Pablo and ask if he'd consider letting me turn his letters into a book.

After some back and forth, we agree that I'll give it a try.

I purchase my plane tickets . . .

Meanwhile, I attend a seminar in Plain City, Ohio, called Helping People in Need. It's mainly for pastors and counselors. I convince myself I should attend because so many people are coming to me for help, but I don't know how to help them.

While there, I realize what a mess I am. One day I leave the seminar, head for a pay phone, and call Mary.

"You don't know how bad it is," I tell her.

We hang up. I drive up and down the streets of Plain City, seriously considering going to a pawn shop, purchasing a gun, and ending my life. Something prevents me.

The next morning I wake up, get down on my knees, and tell God, "I'm done. I can't measure up. This is the last prayer I'll ever pray to you."

I force myself to attend the seminar; I hear a sermon on Rejection and Bitterness. We never get sermons like this in our churches. This one describes me to a T.

Another brother preaches a message on the Ugly Duckling. He describes a little bird who's trying so hard to be a duck, but he can't because he's really a swan. One day he sees a swan soaring in the sky and something stirs inside him. He eventually grows up into a beautiful swan and soars through the skies.

Something strange is stirring inside me. *Maybe I've felt so ugly for all these years because I've been trying to be a duck. But what if I'm not a duck? What if I'm a swan?*

I return home and share some of my experiences with Mary. We both decide I'm too messed up to write Pablo's book. But I've already purchased plane tickets and scheduled the trip.

What should I do?

Chapter 26

HOPE IN THE JUNGLE

Pablo Yoder lives deep in the Nicaraguan jungles. To get to his place, we travel more than eight hours in a four-wheel drive vehicle through greasy, muddy roads—with some ruts in the road so deep we have to look up to see ground level!

Pablo and his family are missionaries in a country recovering from the ravages of a recent civil war. Violence is still rampant. Murders and kidnappings are common, and Pablo and his fellow missionaries have been robbed nearly two dozen times in three years.

When I arrive at Pablo's house, I tell him how messed up I am inside. I'm not sure why I'm here.

I hope visiting a place so intense and violent will crack my depression and let some air into my head. I'm trapped inside myself, overwhelmed with my own hurts. Desperate for relief, I want to be around people with problems bigger than mine.

I'm going to Nicaragua to help Pablo and his friends, but I also hope I'll find some light in my darkness.

Pablo and I pray and ask God if I should help him write his book. Although I'm weak and broken, we both sense God telling us yes, I should help Pablo in this way.

We agree to work on the book together during the day. Because the robberies are so scary—and usually happen at night—we agree to stop writing about scary things at around 3:30 every afternoon.

In the early mornings I stand on Pablo's porch for hours, singing from the Spanish hymnal I helped create. Local people walk past, stopping to listen. I'm inside *my* pain, crying out to God in *their* language. The war is still fresh in the minds of the locals. Robberies, violence, rapes, kidnappings, and murders are daily occurrences in their troubled country. As I sing on the porch, I'm raising up agonized prayers to Heaven through song, and my pain and theirs mingle together.

Pablo and I develop a close friendship as we dive deep into his book. As the time approaches for me to return home, Pablo says, "I need to talk with you before you leave."

What have I done wrong? I know I cause problems wherever I go, and I'm thinking, *Here comes another rejection,* although I don't know what I've been doing wrong.

When the day comes, Pablo leads us along a jungle trail that follows a creek. We find a shady spot under a canopy of spreading trees and sit on two fallen tree trunks facing one another. "Phillip, I see in you a great gift for gaining people's confidence when you first meet them," Pablo says while gazing kindly into my eyes. "That's good. You know how to open people's hearts."

I'm in shock! Pablo, a pastor, sees good in me?

"You have an honesty about you that makes people believe in you," he continues. "You sincerely desire to please God, and I think that draws people to you."

Pablo pauses to let the words sink in, and I'm feeling an unfamiliar warmth inside.

"You know how to bring Scriptures to life in ways that help people understand the Bible better. I think God wants to use you."

> Everything inside me and around me seems to stand still as I absorb this unfamiliar feeling of acceptance and affirmation, cherishing every word as Pablo's kindness embraces me.

Everything inside me and around me seems to stand still as I absorb this unfamiliar feeling of acceptance and affirmation, cherishing every word as Pablo's kindness embraces me.

"You have talked freely about your depression and suicidal thoughts. I believe God is going to heal you someday, but you should seriously consider going on medication in the meantime. I believe once you're healed, God will open doors for you to serve others. You'll have a ministry, and people will want to hear what you say."

Pablo speaks gently as he looks into my eyes with compassion.

What is this? How is it that this man, whom I've learned to respect deeply, perceives good in me? I want inner healing more than anything! And I don't want it for selfish reasons. I want to be healed so I can help other hurting people find healing. Pablo thinks God will heal me! And he's suggesting medication can help me. I'm skeptical because of all the illicit drugs I took in my younger years. Yet if Pablo thinks I should consider medication, maybe I should. Does this mean I can stop trying to heal myself?

"Grow one step at a time, brother," he says kindly, "and someday, God will use you."

A tropical bird cries out in the distance. The air around us is warm and lazy.

"Am I too hard on you?" Pablo asks.

"No." I shake my head, gazing into his eyes while mine pool with tears. "I think I work well with you. You understand what's going on inside me. I envy people like you because you help others. I'm so messed up, all I can do is try to find healing for myself. I'll probably enter Heaven still a cripple."

"Don't think too highly of me," Pablo says, kindly smiling. "I have my own issues to deal with. Phil, look for the needs in people's lives, and help whenever you can. Because you have suffered a lot of emotional pain and abuse, you can empathize with hurting people and hopefully lead them into a genuine relationship with God.

"However," he adds, "sometimes you talk about yourself too much. You want to share your experiences so badly you cut others off. You'll have to learn not to do that. Your story isn't the only one they need or want to hear. They need to talk about their pain. I think as you learn this, your calling will become clearer."

Perhaps this is why people always pull away from me. Instead of listening to them, I talk about myself most of the time.

"What are you sensing?" Pablo asks. "Do you agree with what I'm saying?"

"Yes, I see that in myself. But I don't believe God ever will heal me or use me. I'm broken beyond repair."

We pray together, and Pablo places me in God's hands. I feel close to God, but I also want to dismiss the moment. In my cynical mind I think Pablo is merely telling me what optimistic preachers are supposed to tell hurting people. Surely Pablo can't be saying anything positive about me and mean it!

Yet in a daring, risky move, I whisper to God in the Nicaraguan jungle: "If you ever heal me, I will devote my life to healing others."

* * * * *

When I return to Kentucky, I try to hope for a better future. However, people trapped in depression don't think about the future.

They're imprisoned in the cold, dark tomb of their past and present pain.

But what if my misery has an expiration date? What if I'm on a wilderness path that leads to a Promised Land? Pablo's words leave me daring to hope, and I wonder if maybe God will heal me someday.

Pablo's book, *Angels Over Waslala*, is published in 1997. It sells tens of thousands of copies and inspires many people. Writing for Pablo has been a refreshing opportunity for me to help someone else become successful. In serving Pablo instead of seeking attention for myself, I find a season of relief from my depression.

Taking Pablo's advice to heart, I visit the local library and research my symptoms. I keep coming across the terms *bipolar* and *manic depression*.

I share with my ministers what I'm learning, and I make a bold claim. "I don't want a pill to give me peace. How did godly people overcome manic depression before we had medication? What if my problem isn't medical, but spiritual? The Bible says Jesus heals broken minds.

"Even if I take medication," I continue, "I want to be anointed with oil and pursue God more than I ever have so I can get off the meds as soon as possible."

Unlike my earlier request for anointing in the Tennessee church community, this one is granted without hesitation or heavy ceremony. But my pastors still recommend I see a doctor. A doctor in Ohio diagnoses me as bipolar and prescribes lithium to manage my mood swings.

Next, I believe I need spiritual help beyond what our church offers. The ministers tell me that by seeking help outside our church I'm inferring the church is failing me. Whether that's the case or not, I'm desperate for help, and a counselor in Ohio agrees to help me by phone as his schedule permits. The church leaders reluctantly agree to let me go to a more "liberal" church for counseling.

After a week or two of taking lithium, I'm feeling some relief during the day, but I'm having spasms in my sleep that wake Mary. Another doctor prescribes Trazodone to minimize the tremors. That helps me sleep a little better.

Yet on most nights I'm sleeping one or two tormented hours, then waking up. I wake up Mary, who turns on the light and prays with me. She reads many of the Psalms. No sound is more beautiful than my wife's voice reading Scriptures to me in the middle of my black hell.

I didn't know this until years later, but I'm declaring spiritual war against manic depression, which strangely sounds like demonic oppression. I'm locked in a dark, gray prison inside myself, where there's no hope and no joy. I spend entire days in bed, too emotionally paralyzed to function.

> As I read the Bible, I see promises of light in darkness, healing for broken minds, and a life filled with joy and hope.

Doctors and pastors tell me I'll always suffer from manic depression and need medication. But as I read the Bible, I see promises of light in darkness, healing for broken minds, and a life filled with joy and hope. That means either the Bible is wrong or I'm reading it wrong. I have to find out!

One day I try to pray but only a deep groan and a few halting words come out of me. No *thees* and *thous*. No memorized prayer scripts.

I tell myself, *That's not what prayer is supposed to sound like.*

But a whisper in my heart says, *That was the real you praying to God.*

* * * * *

One day I call Mom and ask, "Was Dad telling the truth when he said we had to move around a lot because I was such a troublemaker?"

"No, Phil. You got into trouble sometimes, but you were a normal kid. You weren't the problem. Your dad was. He was an alcoholic."

I pause for a long moment, aware I'm breathing rapidly. A question stirs deep inside me, but I'm afraid to ask. At the same time, I need to know. I swallow and force the words out.

"Mom, is it true that I'm a monster who will never get along with people?"

"Of course not, Phil. You have a nice personality."

"So why did Dad say that?"

"He was a sick man, Phil."

Her words send shock waves through my mind. I'm not sure if what I'm feeling inside is good or bad, but it's powerful! Through the storm raging inside me, I manage to whisper, "Thanks, Mom. I'll talk to you later."

I hang up the phone, bury my head in my hands, and sob. I've spent most of my life believing I'm a monster who will never get along with people, and that I'll eventually die in a gutter. I've tried killing the monster with drugs, alcohol, and self-hatred. I've hidden him behind my hard Christian shell. I've written and published inspirational articles about the godly man I wanted to think I was. But I never was a monster! I've wasted my life believing a lie. I'm feeling both relieved *and* ashamed.

Now I'm free to learn how to develop healthy relationships with people. But I don't know how or where to start.

At age 47 I need to start over and learn what I should have learned as a child.

Chapter 27

A WOUNDED HEALER

Our Night Sessions continue almost nightly. Because I'm mentally and emotionally paralyzed from my inner pain, I'm not able to pray or even talk. Mary usually prays and reads the Bible to me.

My counselor suggests that reading ten New Testament chapters each day for six months will change a person's life. I'm going to try it. After a few days, it's like I'm banging my head into a concrete wall. I call the counselor and tell him.

"Don't try to study or analyze what you're reading," he says. "Just soak in the Bible."

That works. I can't always handle ten chapters a day, but I read through the New Testament about once every six weeks. Its truth begins to wash away accumulated denominational tumors from my mind, and my emotions begin to stabilize. In addition, some nights I stay awake all night on my knees, praying through Scripture passages.

I also read Psalms where I experience raw, honest emotions with David—pushing through the bitter pain and coming out on the other side praising God. I study Jeremiah, who weeps endlessly at the depth of Israel's sinfulness. As I read Lamentations, I'm absorbing Israel's sins, and I curl into a fetal ball, begging God for mercy for *my* sins for hours on end. I read Isaiah, who sees visions of a day when people with troubled minds get well because God restores them.

These passages penetrate deep into my dark, broken places with light that assures me God understands the pain I can't express in words. As many Scriptures bring light into my dark places, I slowly move toward healing.

Although my intense Bible reading affects me inside in wonderfully positive ways, it's also separating me from the church. This confuses me; I don't know whether to believe the good changes I'm experiencing inside or what the church leaders are telling me, that I just need to submit to the church's rules.

* * * * *

Fall in Kentucky is a beautiful season. Outside, the crickets are holding a steady chorus, but on this mellow night my heart will soon be crushed once again. This evening three ministers come to our house.

We invite them in. We all sit in a circle in our living room. The bishop leans toward me and says, "Phillip, you're way too intense. People are afraid to get close to you." He pauses and looks at the other two ministers; they nod in agreement.

He talks on, trying to convince me something is wrong with me, but I don't need convincing. I already know many things are wrong with me. My pastors are only confirming what my own accusing brain constantly tells me.

"I know what you're saying is true," I explain. "But when I was in Nicaragua, Pablo said he saw good in me. For the first time, someone told me something positive about myself. Why can't you do that? Why can't you see that inside this huge, ugly body and crippled mind is someone desperate for affirmation?"

Placing his elbows solidly on his knees, he leans toward me with greater intensity. "Phillip, we're taking away your church membership privileges. You're still welcome to attend church."

Any hope I have of getting help in this church has tumbled down like a house of cards. Once more, I feel the rejection of the people whose approval I desperately crave.

"This doesn't apply to Mary and the children who are currently church members," the bishop adds kindly, looking at my wife. "We will support them any way we can."

The three ministers stand in unison and step outside into the night air. They're taking something with them—doesn't that something rightfully belong to me? But I can't do anything about it.

Now it's past 10 pm. Mary and I stand facing one another in our bedroom. I wrap my arms around her and say, "I'm so ashamed of all that I've put you through."

She holds me tight and says, "We're in this together."

I didn't expect this response. I thought she would agree with the ministers and confirm what an ugly monster I am. As I think about all the ways I've hurt my wife, I cling even tighter and listen to the night crickets outside the open window.

* * * * *

As I continue megadosing in the Bible, I realize Jesus not only understands my mental suffering, he also experienced it on the cross. He came through that horror victoriously, and somehow, I find hope in believing he can do the same for me.

"I'm starting to experience God's character," I tell Mary. "God's heart is so much bigger than I ever imagined!"

She shares my excitement as I slowly heal.

"I want to help other people experience healing through emotional honesty and soaking in God's Word," I tell Mary.

I tell the bishop about my healing and a growing desire to create a retreat center where broken people can come. He asks me to write it all out, so I type a lengthy letter to our ministers. I describe my struggles and my desire to become a wounded healer for other wounded people. I request their blessing. I'm fired up and ready to go!

"I think I'm finding a reason to live again," I tell the bishop when I give him five neatly stapled copies of the letter. "You know how many people come from the outside and try to join our churches but most of them predictably end up leaving? Or how many good church people experience a tragedy—such as a death in the family or a house fire—and within three years they've left the church? I think I understand why. They don't understand God's loving character. They think they must keep the church rules to find favor with God. They don't understand it's more than keeping rules. It's letting the Bible soak in, praying honest prayers, becoming emotionally honest, and experiencing God more deeply in their inner pain."

"I'll read your letter and give copies to the other ministers," the bishop replies, sounding guarded.

I wait a week. No answer. I think the bishop will talk to me at church on Sunday. He leaves before I can catch him.

I wait a second week.

Finally, I call him.

"Well, what do you think?" I grip my phone tightly.

Long pause . . .

"Are you still there?" I ask into the silence.

"The brethren read your letter." As the bishop speaks in his soft, gentle voice, I know he's getting ready to say something that could hurt. "I thought they would either tell me they agree with your vision or that you're wrong and need to be excommunicated. But they didn't say anything. They simply couldn't relate to it. Phillip, maybe you need to go somewhere else. Your vision seems too different from ours. Our ideas of what God wants for his church don't agree with yours."

I'm wordless, trying to stop my mind from racing. Then I speak weakly. "You mean, you're suggesting we move? Again?"

"You seem to have different ideas than ours, and we think maybe you will be happier somewhere else." Again, the words are kind but firm.

"What you're saying is you don't want to deal with me!" I explode. "Just like my dad; you never wanted me. I'm always in someone's way, wherever I go! Now I'm supposed to sell my home, move my business and my family, and go . . . where? Where should I go?"

I rant awhile longer before the bishop says softly, "I'm only telling you what the brethren said in response to your letter."

This life has no bottom. Every time I think I hit bottom, the bottom drops out once again. How deep is the hole? How far can a person fall?

I know I must press on. Even in the dark night of despair I have to take my best shot at moving toward God.

Resigned to moving again, I ask Mary and the children to create a list of what they want in a church.

"I'll try to find one as close to your preferences as I can," I promise.

I hit the road, traveling thousands of miles by car and plane, visiting other conservative churches. I meet with bishops, deacons, ministers, and regular church members. I explain why I think "outsiders" don't remain with our churches, and why some church people leave after experiencing trauma. I describe my vision for a rural retreat where people find healing from emotional wounds.

"They need someone to help them become emotionally honest, and they need to learn how to apply the Bible to their emotional pain."

Many leaders agree with me, but they say it won't work in their church. They bless me and send me on my way. Many nights I kneel by the bed far away from home and cry myself to sleep.

Chapter 28

ESCAPE BY NIGHT

After several weeks of searching, I find a church in Missouri where the leaders say they agree with my vision to help hurting church people. I bring Mary to visit, and we think we've found a sweet little church with a welcoming spirit.

Meanwhile, our situation in Kentucky is deteriorating fast. One night our five oldest children come home after meeting with the church leaders and tell me, "The pastors have turned against you."

"It's a misunderstanding," I respond. "I'll meet with them and clear everything up."

"Don't do that," my children warn. "They're out to get you, and you'll only make things worse."

I call the Missouri bishop. After talking with our children, he gets on the phone with me. "Phillip, the leaders there are set against you. There's nothing more you can do. You need to get your family out of there."

"You mean like immediately?" I ask.

"Yes."

I don't know if his perception is accurate, or if this is part of my insanity, but I'm so afraid and weary that I leave that night and drive the nine hours to Missouri, arriving around sunrise. One of the church leaders invites me to stay in his home while I look for a property so my family can join me.

* * * * *

Mary makes several trips to Missouri to help me find a new home. We find 57 acres of beautiful rolling meadows tucked out of sight from any neighbors. It's on Bethel Drive—Bethel means "house of God"—and that expresses our shared longing to live in God's presence. We envision a large house in the center of the property with smaller cabins spaced around the perimeter. We hope weary people will come and find rest and healing while staying in those cabins. I'll show them how to pray through the Psalms and find God's peace.

We purchase the property and begin to build a house large enough for our nine children. Around a month and a half after I leave Kentucky, Mary and the children join me in Missouri in a large, rented house. We attend the church, and our children attend the church's private school. They don't have as many written rules here as the churches in Tennessee or Kentucky. We think a church with fewer written rules will offer less distraction from the biblical simplicity we crave.

But despite the new freedoms, something isn't right. Corruption crops up everywhere. I observe undercurrents of troubled marriages, unresolved conflicts, and dishonesty.

I didn't grow up in churches. So now I'm wondering if all churches are hopelessly corrupt.

Some leaders seem more concerned with maintaining their image than with helping their own hurting people. As long as people's personal issues remain unresolved, guilt and fear chain them to the church. We hear sermons about submitting to the leaders while warning against other churches. It's a clear message: leaving our church means we're leaving God.

When I ask for biblical references behind certain church decisions, I get blank stares and answers like this: "Modern issues aren't addressed in the Bible, so the church has to come up with its own rules for a modern world."

"Why do we claim the Bible has answers for every aspect of our lives and then ignore it in our daily lives?" I ask. I get no answers.

I'm struggling with debilitating depression and anxiety and ask church leaders to open the Bible and help me find answers. I get nothing. Where's the warmth and sweetness we felt when we first visited here?

I'm catching wind that the leaders are labeling me a troublemaker, and the old cycle of rejection haunts me once more.

However, I'm grateful the church allows me to pursue my dream of helping hurting people. Whether in person or by phone, I document all my sessions and share my notes with the bishop. He tells me never to counsel young people without their parents' approval. This is good advice, and I agree.

I soon discover from the leaders that I'm not only supposed to help hurting people experience God's love. I'm supposed to persuade them to join our church.

Because of that and many other unresolved issues, we cancel our plans to become church members.

* * * * *

Meanwhile, Mary and I are deeply diving into the book of Galatians. We comb back and forth through the chapters, talking, journaling, and asking people what they think the verses mean. In Galatians 3:3, Paul writes, "How foolish can you be? After starting your new lives in the Spirit, why are you now trying to become perfect by your own human effort?" (NLT)

I'm realizing now that most—if not all—of my Christianity comes from my *efforts*. Where's the joyful knowing I once had that God was with me? Where are the divine encounters I experienced when I first

219

Where are the divine encounters I experienced when I first met God? They're long gone, lost in a haze of external religious performance.

met God? They're long gone, lost in a haze of external religious performance.

I read Galatians 5:4: "For if you are trying to make yourselves right with God by keeping the law, you have been cut off from Christ! You have fallen away from God's grace" (NLT). According to this verse, if I expect to become godly by keeping rules, I'm fallen from grace. The Bible says I'm saved by grace, so if I've fallen from God's grace, this implies I'm lost!

Lost!

I ask several church friends if that's what the verses say. They all agree: "Yeah, that's what it's saying."

Our leaders repeatedly tell us horror stories about people who left the church. Their house burns down. Their marriage falls apart. Children turn to drugs. They get cancer and die horrific deaths. I never know if these stories are true or manipulations to make us afraid to leave.

If they're meant to scare us, they work, because I'm scared. After more than a quarter-century in these churches, I can't imagine a Christianity that doesn't place heavy emphasis on written lifestyle rules intended to keep us from sinning. I love many of our beliefs, but I need a church with beliefs like ours while helping people like me find healing for my broken heart and mind.

One day I'm standing alone on Bethel Drive, pondering my confusion, when something deep inside me stirs. I create a journal entry about these emotions. I entitle it:

Early Signs of the Dawn

Back when I was homeless and wandering alone, some nights I slept under the stars in my old, tattered sleeping bag, which I had stolen from someone. I usually slept soundly until I awoke in the pitch dark, cold and afraid. Too cold for my sleeping bag to warm me, I lay shivering for a long, long time, wondering if the darkness and cold would ever go away. After what seemed like an endless night, I heard faint sounds, like maybe a bird singing. Then I heard two. I wondered if these were night birds. Gradually, I sensed the air getting warmer.

More and more birds began to sing. Was that a little soft light stealing through the darkness? Before long, the sun had risen. The day was warm. The birds were in full concert. My fears had fled.

I didn't have a wristwatch back then. If I had one, when I awoke, cold, shivering, afraid, and alone, I would have known the sunrise was only 30, 60, or 90 minutes away.

So it is with life. When we're in a long dark night of the soul, we try to find warmth in the tattered sleeping bags of our former relationships and religion. In some seemingly random moment we awake, feeling cold, shivering, alone, and afraid. Since no one has ever invented a watch to tell us what hour of life we're in, we don't know how soon the dawn will come or if the sun ever will rise again. We hear a bird's song in the distance and wonder if it's only a night bird or—dare to hope—the night is about to end.

* * * * *

I'm standing in the middle of Bethel Drive, crunching gravel under my feet. My eyes well with tears as I gaze on the beautiful dream house we had designed and built and the cabinet shop where I work with my sons. Surrounded by rivers and national forests, our well-manicured 57-acre plot is truly the place of our dreams. Or is it? For the first time in more than twenty-five years, I'm recalling the bitter cries of my youth and the hunger to find love and reality.

I remember when I told my parents, "I don't know what I'm looking for or whether I'll ever find it. But if I find it, I'll know. And if it doesn't exist, I would rather die searching."

I remember that night at my best friend and heroin dealer Wally's house when I wanted to end my life. He asked if I was lonely, and I remember how his question plunged me beneath my shallow surface life into the dark void of my soul.

I remember months of hitchhiking across the United States, alone and homeless; the cold, lonely nights, wondering if I would die in a gutter like my dad had predicted—and wishing I would die because I was in so much pain.

I remember the plywood cave I made under my bed at the commune we named Planet Earth, where I crawled in and wept convulsive sobs until my body no longer could cry. Even when my tears ran dry, my soul was never done weeping.

In the cool, almost-still breeze, I hear a silent whisper in my heart: *If following me means giving up all this, will you follow me?*

Something inside me snaps and releases tons of weight I have been carrying since . . . I can't remember when. Aloud, I softly reply, "Yes, Lord. It has cost you and me too much to come this far and turn back now."

I know what it could cost me. If I leave the church, I'll likely lose my beautiful wife of twenty-three years and my nine children, all of whom are my reason for living. The thought wants to drive me insane! But the fire, the longing to find God, is burning even hotter.

I don't see how my life can get any darker. But what if I'm almost there and quit now? I have to find God or die searching . . .

If I leave the church, some people will label me a heretic and try hard—and very likely succeed—to prevent my wife and children from going with me.

The churches we tried all offered peace, joy, and a happy home life. But somehow, they aren't working for me. The religious rules feel right, but they never reach the root of my problems. My wife and I have tried everything that should produce a happy marriage, yet something is still wrong.

It's time to look elsewhere for spiritual direction and leadership. I don't know where, but I can't continue the endless, grinding effort to earn God's approval by keeping a set of manmade rules. I must find real life and fulfillment at any cost, even if I lose everything and return to the streets, homeless and alone, as I did more than thirty years ago.

It's like I'm waking up from a long, deep sleep after a cold, dark night. It's morning, and the sun is rising.

When I enter the house to tell Mary, she not only understands, she supports my desire to continue our search for answers.

When we tell our children, some of them simply accept it, while others resist and tell me I'm always searching for healing, and that my healing won't come from a new church.

As we start planning our exit, I discover that one of the church leaders and his wife have often been secretly meeting with some of my children, advising them to separate themselves from their parents. Although I had carefully followed their directive not to counsel young people without their parents' consent, this leader did not follow his own rules. This betrayal leaves me blinded with rage!

This is the final straw! Many of the leaders teach that the church has more authority than the family. Because of that, they make it easy to split families. But I find in the Bible that the father is the spiritual authority over the home—especially when his heart is to serve God. What can I do? Alone, I kneel by my bed and, in God's presence, claim spiritual authority over my family. I don't know if it will work, but I have to try!

A couple of godly friends are helping me navigate this complex maze. They warn me, "Don't say *anything* against your leaders, to your

223

children or anyone. You're out of favor with the leaders, and they can find fault with anything you do or say. If you express any disrespect for them, you'll probably lose your children's respect."

The leaders know how to calmly trigger insecurity and anxiety in me. Then they point to my reactions to convince my children I'm incompetent as a father.

We don't know anyone who left churches like ours without that move dividing the family. Either the parents split or some of the children stay with the church. Despite that dismal record, I'm hoping beyond hope. I tell my godly advisors, "I choose to believe our entire family will get through this. I refuse to entertain doubt because the devil will use those doubts to take us down. I'd rather believe we're all going to make it out and deal with my grief later if we lose one of our children."

For twenty-six years I've placed myself under the authority of churches and church leaders who told me what to believe, how to live, how to run my home, how to operate my business, how to dress, and how to interpret the Bible. Can I walk away from all that? If I come out from under their authority, will I lose my way with God and fall into sin? Can I forfeit the security of "belonging" although I never really belonged? What if the horror stories they're telling us about people who left are true?

What about my children? They don't know another life. Adjusting to a new life could devastate the family.

Is Mary's heart truly with me? She fits into this community socially; I never fit in.

I perceive a clear line in the sand. If we cross it, our lives will never be the same.

Chapter 29

THE EXODUS

Journal entry: August 8, 2000. 4:30 AM

Last night, we stepped into a dark unknown.

Last night, we cut the final thread.

We went to the bishop's house and told him it's time to cut our ties. From now on, please don't consider us part of your church; we want to be neighbors. We love you, but our understanding of the Bible, God, and lost humanity are different. We know you want to help us "outsiders," but you haven't been able to. We want to join ourselves with people who are helping people like me. I know we're very immature at this kind of thing, and I know we'll make a lot of mistakes.

It was so hard to find words last night.

I could have told all the ways I thought he [the bishop] failed me. But God held my tongue. Instead, I told him how bitter I've been toward him and how I spoke evil of him, and I'm so sorry. Mary and the children each shared their hearts. I could feel tugging and tearing in everyone's souls. I could see their hearts bleeding. I felt so low, so dirty, watching all the pain everyone felt because of the decision I had made.

I am a cripple. My emotions have been warped and twisted by the sins of my father and the sins of my own youth. My personality smells bad, and I make many people uncomfortable. I've spent most of the past twenty-six years seeking healing. But God seems to have said no. I came to these people because I thought they could help me. They thought they could help me. Maybe it's all my fault. Maybe I should have tried harder. I don't know. But I never could measure up.

So now we've crossed Jordan. The sun hasn't risen yet. The night is dark, and I feel so alone, so far from home . . .

Oh Jesus, hold me in your arms. I need you so much. I know I won't make it without you. Last night, I saw you alone in Gethsemane, praying for me.

The morning sun rose upon a quiet day. A calm washed over my soul. Our songs in family devotions seemed so close to my struggle. I held back the tears. For our Bible reading we studied Jesus' words in several places where he said, "Follow me." An appropriate beginning to a new day, a new chapter in our lives. Jesus says, "Follow me in spirit, follow me in practical things, follow me in death."

Lord, by your grace, we will follow.

* * * * *

The fallout from leaving the church is swift and painful. It's more like an ugly divorce than a simple decision to find a new church home. For twenty-six years our social circle has been limited almost exclusively to people who look, believe, and think alike. In our isolated communities we believe that people who don't live and believe like us are lost sinners. We even consider our families and relatives heathen with whom we must not associate.

Because we've rejected our families, our children have grown up without grandparents, aunts, uncles, or cousins as part of their lives.

Now that our family has made the decision to leave, we feel alone, so alone. It's hardest for our children, who have never known a different life. Suddenly their friends are no longer permitted to interact with them. When our children press them for a reason, the friends sheepishly repeat a vague rumor about some external change we've supposedly made.

We know these rumors aren't true since we're slow to make any changes. We're not doing the things they say we're doing, but that doesn't matter. When the rumors start, people accept them without questioning. No one checks with us to confirm the truth behind what people are saying about us.

I thought I had counted the cost of leaving, but I wasn't prepared for the endless waves of rejection hitting our family. We're feeling desperate, disillusioned, and even hostile toward God and each other. Although we wish for someone to trust and confide in, we have no one. We're relationally bankrupt. The children are understandably upset by the loss of their friends, and I'm blaming myself for the hard place they're in. We've plunged into a forsaken wilderness.

I've believed in and trusted these people for twenty-six years. This is the only Christianity I've known.

Now what?

We visit mainstream Protestant churches in our community, still feeling wary after decades of brainwashing about the dangers of fellowshipping with anyone unlike us. We're too afraid to trust anyone in any church.

Chapter 30

STEVE, WE LOVED YOU

Shortly after leaving the Mennonites, we attend the funeral of Steve Roberts, a dear friend of the family. Again, God blows holes in our theology.

Steve was a Baptist—not a Mennonite—who smoked cigarettes and watched TV. To my legalistic mind, that made Steve a horrible sinner.

Yet our entire family knew we saw Jesus in him.

Sometimes he would call on the phone just to say, "I didn't have anything to say. I just called to tell you I love you." Steve enjoyed bringing big bags of candy to our children. He would sit in the living room for an hour or two and sing hymns with us.

Sometimes Steve would hug me and tell me how much he loved me. But I'd stiffen up and pull back.

Don't touch me, you filthy sinner! I would think to myself.

Although he knew I looked down on him, he still loved me and was there for me whenever I needed him. When I was really down and out, I'd call Steve, sometimes in the middle of the night, and he would listen to my heart and point me to Jesus. If the church leaders found out I was telling this "heathen" about my struggles, they would punish me for sure! But none of the Mennonites were willing to listen with the same compassion as Steve.

Steve also loved his children. He bragged about his daughter, Mindy. Steve and his sons, Micah and Stephen, traveled the country installing the cabinets we built for Walmart. Wherever they went, they took a day or two off to see the sights.

So now Steve is gone. Several of Steve and Micah's friends have gathered in the church's prayer room. Micah prays in broken sobs: "Lord, I never saw a man love a woman like Daddy loved Mama. Please help me love my wife like that."

Everyone who knew Steve knows about the love Steve and Linda had for each other. He always called her "Miss Leenda," and I never heard him say an unkind word to or about her. When Steve needed a break, he and Miss Leenda headed for a cabin in the Smokey Mountains. Steve would say, "We're going to act like kids for a few days."

It's a most unusual funeral. Before he died, Steve requested that the Holy Spirit be in charge. So the family asked a few men, me included, to sit behind the pulpit and stand up and share anything on our hearts. When I sense it's my turn, I stand before a mixed crowd of about 220 people and bare my heart.

"When we heard that Steve was dying, we were planning to visit him today," I begin. "I had rehearsed what I would say to him. I wanted to apologize. Then, when I heard he died, I was angry with God. But God told me to humble myself and confess my faults publicly.

"Just after I was converted, I did what many of you probably did—I invented my own religion. I took on a form of godliness but lost my connection with Christ. I had licked up my own vomit. For twenty years I lived among you as the worst kind of sinner: a religious one. If I could draw a picture of my soul, here is what you would have seen:

"I looked down on all of you as though I were good and you were evil.

"Given the chance, I would have committed adultery.

"I gave my heart to the selfish pursuit of money and not to God.

"My wife and I often bickered day and night.

"I was angry about something practically all the time.

"I unmercifully beat my children physically and emotionally in the name of God.

"Then, around three years ago, God began to shatter me. I cried out for God's mercy. Not the God of the Mennonites or the Baptists, but the God of the whole earth. And my soul began to heal.

"I know that many of you have a form of godliness. You have the forms of the Baptists, Church of God, Church of Christ, and other denominations. But behind that wall, you're hurting inside. Why don't you come out of your religion and meet Christ?"

Then I ask Mary and our children to come to the stage. We sing "Precious Lord, Take My Hand." Steve would have enjoyed that.

After the service and burial, as people are leaving, Linda's sitting in a folding chair by the gravesite talking with Mary and me. Linda knows I struggle with depression. She looks up at me and says, "Steve got depressed once, several years ago. It made him feel so bad, he decided he'd never let himself get depressed again."

With tears, I tell Linda how bad I feel because I've been such a proud, obnoxious hypocrite around Steve. Linda smiles, looks into my eyes, and says, "Phillip, Steve loved you just the way you were."

"Did Steve know that I saw him as my personal mission project?" I ask Linda.

"Yes. But he knew you would come around when you saw the light."

Lord, I thank you for Steve. He taught us how to love as Jesus loved. Let me have a portion of his spirit.

Chapter 31

A RELUCTANT LEADER

It's 2002. We've left the church that was our only understanding of God for twenty-six years. Without church leaders to submit to, the lot falls upon me to lead our family. Unfortunately, I'm the most messed-up person I've ever known. If I don't know how to lead myself, how can I lead them? As I think about all the failed kings of Israel and Judah in the Bible, I'm drowning in hopeless despair. Are all leaders destined to fail? Are they all corrupted by power and become tyrants who care more about their positions than the hearts of their people? I seriously doubt that anyone is qualified to lead other humans, least of all myself.

More than once, I ask my wife or one of my older sons to lead the family for me. They offer me blank stares. They're waiting for me to step in and lead, but I'm terrified. I don't know how; I have no role models to follow.

Despite our family's pain and my fragile emotions, our business continues to thrive. Our children are becoming adults. We can no longer remain a family business with Dad working alongside his young children. As we consider expanding our business and possibly hiring people, I panic when I think about leading employees. I don't know how to lead people. I only know how to hurt people. This feels like God's cruel conspiracy to force me into a leadership role where I'll inevitably fail.

Then I remember Mr. Baldi, the manager at the clothing store where I worked as a teenager. When I was devastated by the news of Uncle Bert's cancer, Mr. Baldi stood beside me and shared my pain. I don't remember if he said anything. He just stood beside me and let me know he cared.

I think I can do that. I'm too messed up to lead people. I'm afraid I'll destroy them. But I can care about them and sit with them in their pain. I can do that.

* * * * *

I realize to some degree how much pain my children are feeling. A lifetime of teaching about a stern and angry God doesn't evaporate overnight. We've become so immersed in a twisted theology that sorting out our messed-up minds is as impossible as a fish trying to see water.

A pastor who's been observing our journey tells me about a man released from prison after a long sentence.

"So how does it feel to be out of prison?" a friend asks him.

"I'll tell you later," the former convict replies.

A few days later he returns with a glass pop bottle crammed full of copper wire. He smashes the bottle and lifts the mass of wire, still shaped like the bottle.

"This is how it feels to be out of prison," he says.

"Your family is like that wad of wire," my pastor friend explains. "You left the church bottle, but after so many years of getting squeezed into their system, you're still shaped like them inside. Be patient with yourselves. As you pursue truth, you'll be changed to become more Christ-shaped."

His words resonate. I believed our churches were God's elite, but the God they introduced me to shamed me for blowing all my chances of being loved. However, I still faintly believe that Jesus died on the cross for people as messed up as me, and maybe he'll somehow wash away my sins and pain so I can live a pure, clean, and loving life. I can't feel God inside, but I see him somewhere on the distant horizon, and I'm determined to move toward him.

> Now I'm searching for a lesser God who's not as mean and angry as the one I've tried and failed to follow.

In some ways I know I'm more messed up now than *before* I became a Christian. I thought I had failed the great God of the universe, and now I'm searching for a lesser God who's not as mean and angry as the one I've tried and failed to follow.

I'm terrified I'll fall back into sin because I don't have any heavy-handed leaders holding me down or hovering over me to enforce the rules. My thoughts and emotions are so entangled in this legalistic theology that I can't break it—no matter how hard I try. And yet I'm sick of keeping rules while feeling numb toward God.

Every day brings new struggles for our family. Each family member calls or emails someone, reaching out and trying to find someone to help us through our pain. Finally, I ask for a time-out and gather the family together.

"We *all* need help," I acknowledge. "But let's agree on one person to help our whole family."

We find a husband-and-wife team from Colorado experienced in helping abused and traumatized people. They spend a week with us, and I'm not prepared for what surfaces.

After a few days, the husband and wife tell me they sense something "off" about me—perhaps demonic. I radiate a creepy, ominous spirit. They offer their observations so kindly and humbly that I can accept and understand what they're saying. I know how I affect people: whenever I enter a room, they feel something creepy, even if they don't know me. Mary also experiences this from me.

While the wife is helping our children, the husband focuses on helping me honestly look inside myself. I need massive courage and humility for this. My response at one time would have been to shut down and defend myself, but I know I need help!

As the week progresses, I realize I've spent most of my life visualizing myself as a fighter. I'd seen old newsreels of World War II fighter planes engaged in dogfights over England in the Battle of Britain. I've seen myself as a British Spitfire pilot, attacking a German bomber with guns blazing. I'm charging at that bomber so hard that if I don't shoot him down, I'll slam into him, and we'll go down in flames together.

That's how desperately I've been fighting to break the curses from my past. I've been fighting for my sanity all the time. It's been eating me up and creating that creepy, ominous spirit in me.

＊ ＊ ＊ ＊ ＊

Toward the end of the week, I'm beginning to surrender. I imagine Jesus nailed to his cross, and I'm face down in the dirt, my arms wrapped around the cross, restfully clinging to it. Instead of fighting, shouting, raging, and destroying, I surrender my personal war, ammunition, and battle plans to him. I ask him to fight the war for me because it's his job and he's willing to do it.

I experience release.

Peace slowly dawns on my spirit. I'm now opened up enough so we can go deeper and trace my combative spirit back to one pivotal event.

It was that night in Atlanta when I accepted Dad's challenge to fight him.

At first I walked away, as I always had done. But that night, something inside me snapped, and I turned around, walked back to his door, and said I would fight him. At the same time, I knew I had crossed a line by raising my fists against my father.

Although Dad cowered, and we didn't fight, I was fully prepared to fight him. My act of bold defiance invited a demonic, rebellious spirit into my life.

I need to undo that moment, but my dad died twenty-five years ago! I can't go to him and apologize, telling him that regardless of what he did to me, what I did to him was wrong. Instead, I ask God to forgive me for dishonoring my dad, and if he could, to please let Dad know I'm sorry.

New peace washes over me. It is well with my soul.

Now I understand that honoring my parents opens the door for my well-being. While dishonoring my parents may hurt them, I mostly damage myself. Even after my parents are gone, if the spirit of dishonor has infiltrated my being, God says it's not well with me. Furthermore, my children are more likely to dishonor me. It's an unbroken chain.

Thinking about my spirit harming my children makes me realize that my sin against my father could create chaos in them and their relationship with me. I know what I need to do.

I ask Mary to help me meet with each of our children. I apologize to them for how I abused them with my anger, harshness, and failure to express love—all done in the name of Jesus.

Through my tears, I say, "I know what a terrible dad I've been to you. There's no way I can undo all the damage, and I understand how difficult it is for you to forgive me. I only can be sorry and let Jesus

> We weep together, and I hope and pray they're beginning the long process of forgiving their abusive father and finding healing.

pay for what I've done. Can *you* also let Jesus pay for what I've done? If you can't, you may damage your spirit the way I've damaged mine. The cycle will continue down the generations. If you choose not to forgive me, your children probably won't forgive you, and it will keep going."

We weep together, and I hope and pray they're beginning the long process of forgiving their abusive father and finding healing.

Chapter 32

THE GREATER HONOR

Not only do I need healing and reconciliation with my children, but I also need to apologize to my mom and Mary's parents. For so many years we've treated them as wicked sinners. Even when we offer vague "apologies," attempting to reconcile, they sense our condescending arrogance toward them.

We're going to leave our judgment of their spiritual condition between them and God. We dishonored and disrespected them, and we were wrong. We're sorry. No excuses. No explanations.

This causes conflict in me. Most of them don't even claim to be Christians. I've proclaimed myself Mr. Super Christian! What if I confess my sin against them and they interpret that to mean Christianity doesn't work? God will have to sort that out. I've been wrong, and I need to humble myself and sincerely apologize for how I've treated my mom, brother, sister, and Mary's family.

When we come to them that way, we experience an instant shift, and the walls between us come down. Our parents receive us with open arms, as though nothing has happened, and decades of heaviness and hostility between us disappear. Far from compromising our

Christianity, our decision to honor them—no matter what—validates and strengthens God's Spirit in us. We're no longer afraid they might contaminate us. We no longer need to fight them. After two and a half decades, the Prince of Peace has ended the conflict between us.

* * * * *

In 2003, I'm able to be with my mom during the last few days of her life. I feel true respect for her that has been missing for years. Mom has had a stroke and a brain hemorrhage and she's not in her right mind. She claws at whoever is there and cries out, "Help me! Help me! Help me!"

Something odd happens. From my past experiences with LSD, I understand Mom's psychosis. That seems strange, but I can enter her psychosis, come alongside her, and comfort her with my presence. It's as though God has redeemed even my LSD experiences, showing me there's nothing so ugly he can't use once I give it to him.

My mom always enjoyed our family's singing and had asked us to record some music for her. As she sinks deeper into a coma, the recording plays over and over. Songs about families who love each other. These include Thomas Dorsey's "Precious Lord, Take My Hand."

My brother and his wife have lined the room with scented candles. As the candles flicker out one by one, I sense her spirit leaving the room, like incense streaming upward.

I weep and pray. I hold her hand in mine and stretch my other hand upward to Heaven, reaching for God's hand.

"Look to Jesus, Mom," I beg. "He's the hope of Israel."

Then Mom silently slips away. "She's gone," the hospice nurse quietly says. Only a few candles remain, gently flickering in the room.

A few hours later, a female rabbi comes to see us. Later she said she never experienced such a presence of peace in someone's home after a death.

At the funeral, I acknowledge in front of everyone how I dishonored my mother and that I reconciled with her before she died. Then Mary, the children, and I sing a couple of songs.

Afterward, the rabbi hugs me and says, "Whatever you're doing—keep doing it." Even the Jewish rabbi is honoring the peace we're finding in Christ.

* * * * *

For years, Mary's parents planned and paid for memorable vacations for the whole family in places like Europe, Hawaii, or Colorado. But we refused to join them since we viewed them as heathens. In addition, I thought they were wasting money on such expensive vacations.

Now that we're rebuilding relationships with them, we're coming to understand that Mary's parents express love for their children through their generosity. We accept their gracious offer to join the whole family (around thirty people) at a large villa in Tuscany, Italy. Our family flies to Germany and travels through the Alps by train to meet the rest of the family at the villa in a lovely vineyard.

Mary's mom is battling an aggressive cancer and living for this final experience with the entire family. We enjoy our time with them and honor them in every way we can.

I won't pretend switching from harshly judging them to honoring them is easy. The first night in Italy, the darkness in and around me is so thick I can almost reach out and grab it. I've caused great trouble for my wife's family; I've been scornful and proud and said many hurtful things to and about them. Although I've sincerely apologized and been forgiven, my mind is so locked in the harsh judgmental theology we came from that I can't turn it off—even though I want to.

In the pitch-black Italian night, I'm experiencing a fierce internal conflict. My mind wants to scorn and criticize them, but my heart wants to love and respect them. I see my mind so damaged from having been shamed into reading the Bible through the church's interpre-

> I see my mind so damaged from having been shamed into reading the Bible through the church's interpretations that I can't read the Bible with clean innocence.

tations that I can't read the Bible with clean innocence.

I think: *At least when I was living in open sin and doing drugs, I knew it was wrong. But to have my mind so programmed that I read the Bible through twisted interpretations, I'm once again broken—perhaps this time truly beyond repair.*

I pray. "God, my mind is twisted and tangled beyond repair. It's too late for me, but please save my children. Let them read the Bible with clean minds."

God whispers to my heart. *Paul was a Pharisee whose mind also was twisted by legalism. I showed him grace and healed his mind, and I'll do the same for you. Stop trying to fix yourself and let me do it for you.*

Not so easy for me. As a craftsman, I fix stuff. So why can't I fix myself? Although the whisper offers me a ray of hope, I still believe my mind is damaged beyond repair.

"My mind is too broken to fix," I pray. "I need a new mind."

God brings Philippians 2:5 into my thoughts: "Let this mind be in you, which was also in Christ Jesus."

Jesus had a healthy mind. Can I receive his mind?

God healed Paul, whose thinking had been warped by pharisaical legalism. Paul, who used Scriptures to justify hatred and violence against Jesus' followers, received from God a renewed mind in Christ. God will give me that mind too! I'm not asking God for something impossible for him. I know he's willing and ready to do my brain surgery.

I study the broader context in Philippians 2 and read that Jesus didn't create a reputation for himself. Instead, he used his gifts and influence to help others succeed. In contrast, I've been using my gifts to build a platform for myself—I've been using others to help me succeed. I thought God owed me a place of greatness above others because of all I had suffered.

I ask God, "Do you mean if I stop using others to make me successful and give myself to making them successful, I could have a healthy mind?"

I hear God say: *Try it . . .*

God will give me that mind too! I'm not asking God for something impossible for him. I know he's willing and ready to do my brain surgery.

So I shift my focus from using other people to help me become successful. I start using my gifts and talents to help others succeed.

More of the dark, heavy depression begins to lift from my spirit. From that day forward, I build my life on helping other people succeed. As I follow that path, I'm beginning to succeed also.

Chapter 33

"WHAT'S YOUR PURPOSE?"

It's not a once and done thing. It's more of a slow, steady journey. The heavy religious clouds slowly lift from my mind so I can enjoy reading the Bible. I'm starting to enjoy the inner light I experienced when I first heard the Bible read in 1974. The Gospel is becoming simpler, and I experience what Jesus means when he says his yoke is easy and his burden light. The more I'm healed, the more I want to serve God and help broken, hurting people find healing and success in life.

Somewhere in this space in time, after a long six or seven years of intensely pursuing God, the Night Sessions become fewer and less intense, and I'm able to wean off my medication. Long hours of soaking in the Bible and deep, honest, agonizing prayers are doing what the Bible says they will: healing my mind. One day I take my last dose of lithium. On another day I take my last dose of Trazodone.

Encouraged by the couple from Colorado who helped our family, I decide to become a counselor. They recommended a counseling school in Indiana, so I attend their classes, watch their videos, and read their books.

I invite hurting people to spend a week in our house for counseling. Many come and go. One is Roberta, who was raped by her stepfather and went to a Christian counselor, who also raped her. No one could get near her. She was intimidating, but I stuck with her until she broke through.

I'm getting into people's stuck and frozen hearts, watching them surrender their inner garbage to God and come out freer and cleaner.

However, my counseling "ministry" severely overloads the family. People stay in our house for a week at a time. While trying to meet their needs, we're trying to keep our cabinet business going. All nine children are still at home, and Gina and the girls cook everyone's meals, do everyone's laundry, and try to keep our home atmosphere sane.

(At this point in my story, it's important to mention that our exodus having been made, Mary returns to Gina, her original name.)

Some people bring their heavy religious baggage and criticize Gina and the children for absurd details like the length of their sleeves. Not wanting to offend our visitors, I side with them against my wife and children, alienating my family.

After several months, Gina says, "I can't do this anymore! It's insane!"

She and the children are coming unglued. We've lost our privacy. With good intentions, we're focusing on people's demons and pain instead of Christ. After they leave, these people call me at all hours of the night and day, driving me to my wit's end because I don't know how to help them.

Still, I want to serve God with all my heart. So I make a list of possibilities:

- Pastor

- Worship ministry

- Missionary

- Counselor: I tried that, and it didn't work.

I try pastoring a home church with a few other families, but we're so heavily indoctrinated from our past that we can't accept anyone who differs from us. We argue over the minutiae of doctrines and practices. People leave because confrontations are so intense.

I guess God doesn't want to me to be a pastor. What if I start a family worship ministry? We purchase several guitars, an electric bass, a violin, and a flute. Gina and I are the only ones in the family who can play a little. Everyone's taking lessons, and we all sing—in the Mennonites, we had been singing a cappella for twenty-six years. I get a full, professional PA system and a small recording studio. Local churches invite us to lead worship, and a businessmen's organization in Chicago pays us to lead a worship evening for them. But behind the scenes, I drive my family so hard to practice and bully them until they want nothing to do with either music or me.

We visit churches in Mexico and Costa Rica, hoping I'll be invited to the mission field. Life is simpler in these countries, as I remembered from my student days in Mexico, and US missionaries are generally respected. But those doors never open.

> My friend Wally had rocked my world many years earlier with a simple question: "What's your purpose?" Decades later, I'm still trying to answer that question.

My friend Wally had rocked my world many years earlier with a simple question: "What's your purpose?"

Decades later, I'm still trying to answer that question. Through all my restless efforts to create some kind of ministry, I sense God telling me, *Don't define your calling.* He often reminds me of his promise to Abraham in Genesis 15:1: "I am your exceedingly great reward."

I'm disappointed by what I sense God is telling me.

Anyone can be saved, I'm telling myself. *I've been through so much. I need a bigger reward, like a platform that insulates me from getting hurt anymore, where people look up to me and give me the recognition I never got when I was a child.*

Again, I hear the persistent whisper in my heart: *Don't define your calling. I am your exceedingly great reward.*

Deep inside, I'm craving a ministry that validates me instead of a place where I can simply serve whether I'm noticed or not. As each of my "ministry" efforts collapses, I keep returning to the one thing that doesn't fail: my woodworking business.

Working with wood is the greatest mental and emotional therapy I know. I can fashion something beautiful from rough materials the same way I want God to create something beautiful in me. People love what I create for them. At the same time, my children are learning trades that will help them become productive with their lives.

My intense, driving personality fits better in business than church or some other ministry. I've been meeting high-profile people from Walmart or multi-billion-dollar construction companies and freely talking about God during our meetings.

I'm starting to get God's message.

I gave God my list of what it means to be a passionate Jesus follower: missionary, counselor, worship leader, pastor. However, everything I've tried has failed. I never saw "working in a business" as an option for a passionate Jesus follower.

> I finally accept I'm not supposed to decide my calling. God calls, I respond.

I finally accept I'm not supposed to decide my calling. God calls, I respond. Business, where I'm succeeding despite my struggles with feelings of inadequacy, where I think God has banished me because I flunked out of the church, is where God is calling me. His calling has already been with me, but I don't discover it until I reach the end of my failed ambitions.

I asked God for a position in the church; meanwhile, he's sending big companies to my door asking for cabinets.

Every God-serving option has closed to me—except one. *"This door, Lord? Are you sure this is where you want me to go?"* I ask.

Step forward. You'll see.

After I "flunked out" of religion, I entered a new world that he has prepared for me, where I can fit in and make a difference. Three decades after I met God in the Tennessee woods and began to follow Jesus the carpenter, I finally understand my calling. I'm meant to do the one thing I've repeatedly succeeded at and found fulfillment in: leading a business where people are working with wood.

While the churches I attended have been falling apart, business is where I find my sanctuary, where I often fall on my face and beg God to help me build cabinets that please my customers.

It doesn't look or feel like a ministry, but I sense God created me for this, and people who know me are confirming it. Something remarkable happens as I embrace this truth and invite God to run the business for me. I've spent my life desperately trying to earn recognition, approval, and applause. When I stop pursuing that and approach woodworking as God's calling for me, success follows. I win national recognition and awards.

For example, in 2017 I'm invited to Washington, DC, where I'm recognized as the Small Business Association's Small Businessperson of the Year for Missouri. In addition, our company and I are featured in the *Saint Louis News* and *Forbes* magazine for our amazing culture that puts people and their families ahead of profits.

As our company grows, I hire people who are as broken as I have been, giving them the opportunities I had often been denied. As a result, many of them find the same peace and fulfillment working with their hands that I had discovered.

I spend many long hours reading the Bible and praying, searching for ways to incorporate the Bible into our workplace. Although we respect everyone's beliefs (or lack of beliefs), Cohen Woodworking unapologetically becomes a Christian company. We provide resources for our employees to build healthy families, learn money management skills, and improve themselves in many other ways. We have a chaplain for employees wanting deeper spiritual guidance.

At each growth stage I've doubted myself and questioned whether I could lead the company I founded. On more than one occasion I give my leadership team the opportunity to replace me, fully expecting they'll do so. Instead, they express their support and ask me to continue as CEO. I call that leading by permission, inspired by Jesus' example. He only leads people who invite him to lead and guide them.

Although Cohen Woodworking is a for-profit business, it also has been my ministry for many years. I've been transformed to greater heights and greater depths of knowing Jesus by humbly inviting him to lead me and our company, and I've watched many employees' lives be transformed as well.

> Although many of them don't understand this, I tell them, "You're also saving my life."

Many people working for me tell me I'm saving their life. Although many of them don't understand this, I tell them, "You're also saving my life."

* * * * *

Now I'm in my early seventies. In 2021 I transitioned out of the company and into what the business world calls retirement. It's been a bittersweet transition. I spent most of my life in a restless search for acceptance, fulfillment, and success. It took many decades before I discovered the answer to Wally's question: "What's your purpose?" When at I last realized I was meant to be on this earth to be a craftsman for God's glory—to shape beautiful pieces of craftsmanship from wood and to labor with God to help shape broken lives—I experienced peace and satisfaction I had never known before.

That happy period feels like a short season of my troubled life, but I thank God I was able to experience it.

My journey continues. I want to enjoy both my natural and spiritual children and grandchildren and want them to enjoy me. I want to grow closer to Gina, and I want her to know how I treasure her partnership on this journey. I want to experience adventures with her, traveling, playing music, and worshiping together.

I want to help business owners learn how to invite Jesus into their hearts and companies. I want to pass this book to my children and grandchildren as a record of God's kindness to our family despite my failures. I want readers of my story to understand the incredible gift of grace and freedom God offers once you give him complete control. I want to bask in the love and acceptance of my heavenly Father after decades of believing that wasn't possible.

Yet the battle isn't over. Our enemy knows that we're remembered, not only by how we lived, but by how we *finish*. The temptations and attacks on my soul are sometimes fiercer now than ever.

When I was in Nicaragua, I promised God that if he healed me, I would give my life to healing others. He healed me, and I've kept my promise for more than twenty years.

Yet sometimes God asks us to remain faithful and serve others even if he doesn't heal us.

Faithful to the end . . .

Epilogue

JESUS SHINES THROUGH

In 2020, Gina and I decide to take adventures we call Friends and Beauty. The idea is simple: we visit friends and appreciate the beauty in their lives and where they live. For our first experience we visit our friends Jeff and Kerry in Salt Lake City, Utah.

Some years earlier, during a difficult season at our woodworking company, several people advised me that we needed better accountability in our culture. When I contacted the people at The Oz Principle, an organization that teaches workplace accountability, they connected me with Jeff, one of their facilitators.

I soon learn Jeff has gleaned a wealth of wisdom from many years in his family's business, and he's also helping us with those insights.

Jeff becomes one of our "mountain guides"—someone who has crossed the mountains we're facing and knows the way. So rather than stumbling along and learning from our mistakes, we have the privilege of following Jeff as a guide.

In addition to helping our company, Jeff and I become friends. Like the family in New Mexico that had impressed me during my hitchhiking days, Jeff attends a Mormon church. I must wrestle with the question: how can I overcome my prejudices about his religion and still remain faithful to the biblical Jesus I have come to know?

As we get to know each other, Jeff and I expand beyond business and talk about our personal and family lives, including following Jesus and letting the Bible guide us. While Jeff is teaching us about creating accountability in the workplace, I share with him what I'm learning from the Bible and my journaling dialogues with God.

So, as part of Friends and Beauty, Gina and I travel west to visit Jeff and his family. We're becoming friends, but I'm also somewhat guarded about some of our major differences in beliefs. And yet, still deeper, I know we share a desire to know Jesus and follow him. I'm trying to keep an open mind and simply appreciate the beauty in Jeff's life and family. They welcome us graciously and invite Gina and me to play music and lead their family in worship and Bible study during the evenings.

One day Jeff and Kerry take us on a tour of the Mormon temple and other famous sites in Salt Lake City. After lunch they're getting ready to take us back to our hotel. But then I look at Gina and say, "You want to go on an adventure?"

"Sure. What are you thinking?"

"Jeff, you and Kerry head for the house," I say. "We're going to hang out here. We'll Uber back and see you at suppertime."

We wander around Temple Square. We meet a man who explains in depth some of the history of the Mormon church. It's both fascinating and very strange.

After an hour or so, we're sitting on a concrete bench, watching the crowds walking around the square and streaming in and out of the temple, I flash back to that Mormon family in New Mexico. I remember their sincere love and appreciation for each other, and how deeply I admired their family. Now I'm seeing dozens of Mormon families that remind me of them.

At the same time, I'm troubled by the theological gulf that separates Mormons from evangelical Christians. Am I not obligated to confront the errors in their beliefs? As I wrestle with this question, I experience a strange yet wonderful insight.

Suddenly, I don't see Mormons walking in that square. I see beautiful people made in God's image with hopes, fears, and struggles like mine. I guess some of them are passionately seeking Jesus while others have settled into empty religious routines of rule- and ritual-keeping that fail to satisfy. I identify with both groups because I too have been both a religious zealot and a passionate Jesus follower.

I hear a whisper in my spirit.

"Jesus shines through."

Jesus shines through? I think, *He doesn't shine through manmade religious systems and misguided beliefs, does he?*

"That's not for you to worry about," the voice whispers to my heart. "Like every denomination and religious group you've belonged to, this one has corruption and strongholds too entrenched for you to conquer. Don't judge. Instead, look for Jesus to shine through the most unlikely people and places. He is too big to be confined to those with 'perfect' doctrines. Once they invite Jesus' light inside them, his light will lead them where they need to go."

I'm sitting in silence trying to make sense of this message. Has Jesus really shined through imperfect people with wrong beliefs to reveal himself to me?

And then, in a tender moment of revelation, I know he has. Yes, of course he has! Over and over, the people and experiences in my life have given me glimpses of Jesus, even when I don't recognize him at the time . . .

My mind drifts back to the dark memories of my early childhood. I shudder as I remember the fighting, screaming, spitting, and drunken beatings. And then Uncle Bert's smiling face and firm handshake appear in the stream of grim memories. My heart glows as I recall his unconditional love and acceptance, and I understand—Jesus, the source of love, loved me through Uncle Bert! In the dark horrors of my childhood, Jesus gave me a glimmer of hope through one man who loved me as Jesus loved: unconditionally.

Then I remember Mr. Baldi, the boss who silently shared my grief and expressed his care when my heart was breaking over Uncle Bert's terminal illness. As I relive that scene, I sense Jesus standing in the shadows behind Mr. Baldi, wiping tears of compassion from his eyes as he loves me through the simple kindness of my boss.

There was that day as we were driving through the Mexican countryside when I was weeping as I saw simple peasants living in poverty and yet happy. Now I sense Jesus walking among those humble people, smiling as I weep and wonder about the mysteries of their happiness and the breathtaking beauty of the Mexican Rockies.

Tears spill from my eyes as I relive one scene after another, realizing for the first time that Jesus was there. He was with me as I experienced the love of a humble family on a New Mexico ranch. Jesus arranged that encounter, putting a hunger in my heart that I never lost.

Now I see myself standing beside the road, somewhere in Oklahoma or New Mexico, thumbing rides to California. As I gaze at the western horizon, I imagine arriving at my destination and the better life it promises. In a whispered moment of understanding, I know I'm created to be a visionary, one who's always seeking a better world.

I see Jesus smiling on a quiet, lonely street in Blacksburg, Virginia, as I meet Gina for the first time, and I know our meeting is no random accident. He's guiding Gina and me toward each other just before midnight on the day I believe I'll meet my future wife. She's the greatest of all my treasures and God has used not only her beauty and virtues, but her flaws as well, to give me a greater hunger to be more like Jesus so I can be worthy of her love.

The scene shifts to a rundown county jail in Altamont, Tennessee, where a stern-faced sheriff leads me to my jail cell. He pauses, looks into my eyes, and says, "I have faith in you. I think you can make it." I see Jesus speaking through the sheriff, smiling and nodding in agreement. Jesus too had faith that I would make it.

I remember discovering the joy of woodworking, the therapy of taking rough materials and turning them into beautiful furniture and cabinets. Woodworking has been a bright spot in the darkest periods of my adult life, and now, for the first time, I understand why. Jesus was standing in the background as I worked, appreciating the quality of my workmanship and nodding his approval.

The scene shifts to a tiny jungle clearing where I sit on a log, facing Pablo Yoder, a man I've come to deeply admire and respect. Instead of the criticism and condemnation I expect from a preacher, Pablo speaks life and the hope of healing into my wounded spirit. That's *Jesus* speaking through Pablo, whispering what he can do with a person like me who's been broken into many pieces—first by sin and then by religion.

I feel Steve Roberts hugging me and telling me he loves me while I stiffen myself and resist him because he doesn't fit my definition of a Christian. So many times—against the approval of my church elders—I call him in the middle of the night and pour out my pain, and he tells me how much Jesus loves me.

Jesus can shine through in every workplace, family, prison, nursing home, place of worship, ghetto, concentration camp, mansion, palace, or individual—when we sincerely and honestly invite him in.

I see Jesus shining through the pain and trauma of my childhood, the years of desperate searching, loneliness, and rejection, and even in the frailty and chastisements of growing old.

Jesus was shining on me and in me when something inside me lit up the first time I heard the Bible read. And despite all the darkness of human religion, he's still shining in me whenever I quietly sit and read the Bible.

I now realize that the worst prison isn't certain denominations, seemingly impossible circumstances, past trauma, addictions, or long-standing unbroken family iniquities.

The worst prison is to be trapped inside my head without seeing Jesus. But when I lift my heart and let him in, he shines through.

Jesus can shine through in every workplace, family, prison, nursing home, place of worship, ghetto, concentration camp, mansion, palace, or individual—when we sincerely and honestly invite him in.

Oblivious to the crowds surging around me in Temple Square, I lift my eyes to Heaven and whisper, "Thank you, Jesus! Even when I feel lonely and abandoned, you are here, shining through unlikely people and circumstances to let me know I'm not alone. Thank you for always being there and here. Thank you for shining through."

* * * * *

Dear Reader,

Now you've journeyed with me through my story. You see how I've pursued God hard for more than fifty years, searching for the God who heals and for people who truly love each other. It's been painful and glorious, fraught with pain, rejection, betrayal, failure, and success.

When I was abused as a child by my own father and hated by the world around us because I was born into a Jewish home.

When I was homeless, poor, and suffering through many rejections, betrayals, and dark nights of the soul.

When I was doing well and using my wealth and influence to help those who were down and out.

Jesus was shining even when I couldn't see him. I remind myself to look for him each day to shine through some of the least likely moments, people, and places in my life. And I want him to shine *through* me, one of the least likely people to bear his image.

The sorrows of aging sometimes hit me with wave after wave in their fullest fury. Family conflicts. Tired, aching mind and body.

Friends who turn away from God. People around me dying. I recently was diagnosed with macular degeneration. I'm slowly losing my eyesight. I was anointed and prayed over by the church elders for my healing. God can heal me or choose not to. Yet I'm not afraid as I meditate on Isaiah 42:16: "I will bring the blind by a way that they knew not; I will lead them in paths that they have not known: I will make darkness light before them, and crooked things straight. These things will I do unto them, and not forsake them."

I know that even if my eyes stop seeing, Jesus will find ways to shine through to me. And I know I will see him and Heaven someday soon, with clear eyes.

So my dear reader friend, you've journeyed with me through my story. Invite Jesus into your story. Pursue God with everything in you so you can finish well. And meet me sometime, either here on earth, or in eternity with him.

Love and Grace,
Phillip Cohen

ABOUT THE AUTHOR

Phillip Cohen founded Healthy Leaders, an organization that helps struggling business owners build strong, cohesive leadership teams with God in the center. His talks, workshops, seminars plus his frequent podcasts carry his message of bringing Jesus into life, often in unexpected ways and places. This theme and opportunity are now also shared through his book revealing his own life and struggles.

Phillip grew up in inner-city Chicago, Atlanta, and Miami before settling in rural Tennessee with his wife after wandering around in three countries. In the early 1970's he discovered a talent for woodworking and started Cohen Woodworking in 1982, which eventually gained multiple contracts with large clients such as Walmart. In 2017, Phillip was awarded the Small Business Person of the Year for Missouri. In addition, the company was featured in many news stories and media outlets for placing people ahead of profits. Phillip retired in 2021. Two of his sons, Ben and Nate, currently run the business. He resides in Central Missouri.

To learn more about Phillip Cohen and his work and ministry, go to www.Healthy-Leaders.org and www.JesusShinesThrough.com